The Mystifications of a Nation

The Mystifications of a Nation

"The Potato Bug" and Other Essays on Czech Culture

VLADIMÍR MACURA

Translated and edited by Hana Píchová and Craig Cravens

THE UNIVERSITY OF WISCONSIN PRESS

Publication of this volume has been made possible, in part, through support from the ANONYMOUS FUND OF THE COLLEGE OF LETTERS AND SCIENCE at the University of Wisconsin–Madison and from the CZECH CHAIR FOUNDATION of the University of Texas at Austin.

The University of Wisconsin Press
1930 Monroe Street, 3rd Floor
Madison, Wisconsin 53711-2059
uwpress.wisc.edu

3 Henrietta Street
London WCE 8LU, England
eurospanbookstore.com

1   3   5   4   2

Printed in the United States of America

Library of Congress Cataloging-in-Publication Data
Macura, Vladimír, 1945–
The mystifications of a nation: "the potato bug" and other essays on Czech culture / Vladimír Macura; translated and edited by Hana Píchová and Craig Cravens.
        p.   cm.
Includes bibliographical references and index.
ISBN 978-0-299-24894-9 (pbk.: alk. paper) — ISBN 978-0-299-24893-2 (e-book)
1. Czech Republic—Civilization. 2. Czechoslovakia—Civilization.
3. Czechoslovakia—Intellectual life. 4. Czech Republic—Intellectual life.
I. Píchová, Hana, 1961– II. Cravens, Craig Stephen, 1965– III. Title.
DB2035.M33   2010
943.71—dc22
2010011537

Contents

Illustrations

Semio-Feuilletons on the End of Empires

The Cult of the Center and the Comedy of the Bridge

CARYL EMERSON

Semioticians love to demystify myths, thereby disabling them, and Vladimír Macura is no exception. As a creative writer, however, he knows that disabling alone is not a satisfactory endpoint. Some new paradox or mystery must be set up along the way—if only to keep the reader's attention and ensure that the text continues to live. One such paradox is deftly structured in to the present book, between two potent symbols: chapter 4 on the Center and chapter 6 on the Bridge.

From Johann Gottfried von Herder, patron saint of ethnic diversity, through the nineteenth-century Czech National Revival, to the impassioned "small-nation chauvinism" of Milan Kundera in the 1980s, the concept of Central Europe (often with Prague as its center of centers) has signified creative synthesis. This tidy city, we are told, is the beating heart of the organism, the mediator, the true golden mean, that which discredits the frantic extremities of "edge peoples" and cultivates the sober, "sensible freedom" of a cosmopolitan core. If residents of the Center do wander to the periphery, like Jaroslav Hašek's Good Soldier Švejk during the Great War that brought down the Austro-Hungarian Empire, they do so with the durability and solidity of a Josef Lada cartoon, whose unforgettable unflappable hero is never properly shaved and always on the lookout for the nearest pub. Such is good-humored *českost* or "Czechness," a reality-check on all utopias.

But then there's the Bridge. Unlike the Center, which is absorptive and accretive, bridges are expected to lead somewhere. People rush over them, carrying goods to vital destinations; when a bridge comes down, communications are cut and each side defaults to its earlier provincial language, products, tempo, and prejudice. Symbolism is most intense when the structure connects two distinctly different places or things. Prague has its magnificent Charles Bridge, of course, but probably the most famous Central European bridge is somewhat further south, the structure that gave its name to Ivo Andrić's Nobel Prize–winning epic novel *The Bridge on the Drina* (Na Drini Čuprija), published at the end of the

Second World War. This glorious 400-year-old edifice in northern Bosnia was born in violence (among its early memorable scenes are sixteenth-century Turkish authorities impaling a Slavic peasant who would dislodge its stone foundations), but the bridge eventually triumphs and civilizes. It connects a myriad of cultures and trade routes, its vendors serving coffee to Muslims, Turks, Orthodox Slavs, Jews, Italians, and Austrian occupiers alike. A successful bridge can become a center. By the final chapter of the novel, however, the bridge over the Drina at Višegrad has been mined and dynamited; the year is 1914. Such is not the metaphysical Czech Bridge invoked by Macura in his essay "The Bridge."

Macura opens that essay with a reference to Václav Kliment Klicpera's 1826 play *Comedy on the Bridge*, concerning "two people stuck on an unnamed bridge above an unnamed river in an unnamed land." They are "unable to cross over or return because soldiers of enemy armies have closed both sides of the bridge." The comedy is potentially surreal and black. In fact, Macura's one-line plot summary suggests Danis Tanović's acclaimed 2001 film, *No Man's Land*, in which a Bosnian and a Serb, survivors in a trench during the most recent Balkan War, eventually manage to murder one another behind an ineffective United Nations tank that had been called in to defuse a lethal bomb. Klicpera does not take this route, however. His play about two people stranded on a bridge is neither nationalistic nor militant. Although the play is a farce, Macura assures us it "does have something essential to say: perhaps about the banality of everyday human problems against the background of historical events, or, on the contrary, about the nonsensicalness of historical mechanisms against the background of human everyday life."

This casual two-way comment on Klicpera's trapped bridge-dwellers is emblematic of Macura's cultural criticism as displayed in this anthology. It also provides a clue to its distinctiveness when measured against the Russian semiotician whom Macura invokes as predecessor and inspiration: Yuri Lotman (1922–93). Although he was a dissident scholar working in Tartu, Soviet Estonia, far from the closely watched Soviet center, Lotman was nevertheless writing about, and within, an empire. To explicate its expansive and repressive structures, he and his fellow semioticians worked up seriously ambitious binary constructs that juxtaposed Russian to "Western" (that is, non-Russian) concepts of space, time, progress, and justice.

A history of the movement published by Maxim Waldstein in 2008 is suggestively titled *The Soviet Empire of Signs*—and indeed, that could be the legacy of semiotics. Near the end of his life, Lotman appeared to soften the imagery of the Tartu School by introducing the breathing, organic notion of a "semiosphere." Still, a big-nation, big-influence aura clung to the project: an *empire* of signs. Waldstein confronts this issue directly in a section of his chapter 6 titled "Tartu Culturology and 'Imperial' Semiotics." "Semiotic imperialism" comes in two forms, Waldstein explains. The first is more general, "the desire by semioticians to claim expertise over almost any field of knowledge on the basis of the assumption that semiotic mechanisms take place everywhere" in all fields of scientific inquiry. The second reading of "imperialness" is more specific to Lotman's Soviet school. There is no racism, no domination of one nation-state over another; quite the contrary. Tartu scholars claim that "human culture cannot be modeled on the ethnically based and linguistically homogeneous nation-state or on the ethnicity-blind 'republic.' Rather, the Tartu Empire of Signs is a multinational and multi-lingual realm . . . a syncretic and polyglot space where multiple incommensurate discourses enter into dialogue with one another in an effort to build bridges across the multitude of symbolic and material borders that constitute the semiosphere." Waldstein suggests that Lotman, nonconformist Soviet-era intellectual, had an imperial agenda concealed under all this talk of polyglossic bridge-building intended to interconnect disparate realms of a semiosphere. His real models, Waldstein hazards, were the "Holy Roman Empire, Austria-Hungary, the British Empire"—and now, of course, whatever government dominates the Eurasian land mass, the biggest contiguous stretch of territory on earth.[1]

Other critics of Lotman's big-system thinking have gone further. Vladimir Alexandrov, for example, has claimed that Lotman's scientistic attempt to seek grounding for his new, organicist semiotics not in physics but in evolutionary biology is problematic because biological organisms have vastly more complex rules for interaction and combination, rules that *emerge* only at higher levels of hierarchy, thereby enabling the absolutely new. Alexandrov also makes the point that the implicit theory of meaning-production in semiospheric models "pertains to a Western conception of developmental psychology" (especially as regards exchanges between self and other) that cannot and should not be considered globally applicable to all the diverse cultures of the world.[2] Imperialism in this case is not a matter of bayonets, gunboats, or the capitalist financial network, but more simply the assumption on the part of thinkers from one part of the world that their theories and frameworks did not arise locally, out of their own limited conditions and experiences, but are somehow the universal case, the truth at the center, of which the mind of this particular theorist just happens to be the carrier.

There is none of this imperial self-confidence in Macura's semiotics—and in the shadow of Lotman's Tartu School, the essays in this book stand out marvelously humorous and small. Compare, for example, the massive literary mythologem of imperial Saint Petersburg, whose codes are elaborated with great intricacy by Lotman and Vladimir Toporov in the 1970s as part of an emerging school of "urban semiotics," with Macura's essay on Prague (chapter 5). Macura gives us an urban worldview, the Vltava River with castle and tower, but he opens not on such heroic stone structures but on messier, more picturesque nature and village stage comedies. Flowers are an organizing principle in this book. The blossom-bestrewn imagery of the National Czech Revival (chapters 1 and 4) is linked with the myth of the blooming village of Prague (chapter 5), which resurfaces in the enthusiastic Czech assimilation of the Stalinist myth of Ivan Michurin (chapter 11), a horticulturalist who developed "over 300 new types of fruit trees and berries" in the Lamarckian spirit of the geneticist Trofim Lysenko. Macura smiles on this need to turn Czechs into green orchard-dwellers. His discussion of the Prague Metro (chapter 10) is surprisingly somber, pointing out a tension between "above and below, light and darkness," descent into the underworld (even for the pragmatic purpose of speedy transit) that could not easily be integrated into the reigning sunlit myth of the city. (It is instructive to compare this Czech anxiety with the transfigurative epic rhetoric of the Moscow Metro under construction in the 1930s: there the underworld is abolished, for imperial light could vanquish darkness.) Macura states outright that the myth-building impulse in any nation is a "mystification" (chapter 2)—not in the sense of forged documents or faked literary pasts, but simply as an inner need to construct some system that coheres and whose identity one can "put on." Small, repeatedly conquered or colonialized peoples surely need such clothes more than empires do. And it is characteristic of Macura to affirm that "the borders between authenticity and fraud are not as sharp as the borders between a game and a joke."

Finally, in chapter 14 on "Minus-Stalin," the modestly smiling theorist in Macura comes together with his great literary compatriots Václav Havel and Bohumil Hrabal. "Juri M. Lotman coined the term *minus-priem* or 'minus-device' to describe a phenomenon in the world of human creations and ideas in which absence is not always absence," Macura writes. Remove an expected cadence or rhyme in a familiar structure, and one can *hear* the lack, louder even than the thing itself. When the Stalin monument came down off Letná Plane, it made that sort of semiotic noise. This sound was highly specific, particular only to this Czech ethnos and national experience, and whatever goes up on that blank space will have to contend with its echo. Possibly, the advantage of the semio-feuilleton over the semiosphere lies precisely in this particularity. Stories aren't cosmic science but merely sites of witnessing, and when they change (rise, fall, decay), they can be collected and shared, not only discredited or banned. Macura is a Czech bridge.

Translators' Preface

Vladimír Macura's oeuvre is vast, and in order to introduce the English reader to his work on Czech culture—specifically how certain cultural phenomena arose and continued to influence the culture to this day—we have chosen fifteen of his essays to translate, which we think provides a representative sample of his work on Czech culture. These essays, originally collected and published in four volumes during Macura's lifetime, vary greatly in length and style. Specialists will find the longer semiotic essays dealing with the myths and emblems of the nineteenth century especially of interest. The much shorter essays—which Macura refers to as semi(o)-sketches—that deal with the Communist past and the post-Velvet Revolution era have a universal appeal.

Summaries precede each of the essays to place the works in their historical contexts. Further explanatory material is located in the footnotes of the essays. The numbered endnotes are Macura's own and primarily concern the sources he consulted.

Two of the essays have been slightly abridged—"Prague" and "Dream of Europe"—with a wider audience in mind.

We would like to thank the University of Wisconsin Press for supporting this project. We would also like to thank Naděžda Macurová for permission to publish these translations, which originally appeared as follows: "The Center" and "Prague" in *Znamení zrodu: České národní obrození jako kulturní typ* (Sign[s] of the birth: The Czech National Revival as a cultural type) (Prague, 1995); "Dream of Europe" in *Český sen* (The Czech dream) (Prague, 1998); "Michurin," "The Potato Bug," "Spartakiad," "The Metro," and "Death of the Leader" in *Šťastný věk: Symboly, emblémy a mýty 1948–1989* (The joyous age: Symbols, emblems and myths, 1948–1989) (Prague, 1992); "Mystification and the Nation," "Where Is My Home," "The Bridge," "Symbol with a Human Face," "Renaming," "Minus-Stalin," and "The Celts within Us" in *Masarykovy boty a jiné semi(o)fejetony* (Masaryk's boots and other semi[o]-sketches) (Prague, 1993).

HANA PÍCHOVÁ and CRAIG CRAVENS

Introduction

The Czech World of Vladimír Macura

PETER BUGGE

Vladimír Macura (1945–99) was a versatile and prolific scholar, and his innovative studies in Czech literature and culture from the National Revival of the early nineteenth century to the Stalinist era and beyond have had a lasting impact in his native country in a wide range of disciplines: literary history and theory, semiotics, cultural studies, and history, among others. Articles of his have been translated into English, German, French, Polish, Slovak, and other European languages, but the present volume constitutes the first comprehensive presentation of his work outside the Czech Republic.[1]

Macura was also a diligent translator of Estonian literature into Czech and a gifted writer of prose fiction, and in October 1998 he was awarded the Czech Republic's State Prize for Literature. In an unprecedented but fitting gesture, the prize committee chose to honor Macura both for his novel *Guvernantka* (The governess, 1997) and for his collection of scholarly studies *Český sen* (The Czech dream, 1998). In this way, they recognized the literary qualities of Macura's scholarship and highlighted the close, almost symbiotic relationship between scholarly meticulousness and poetic creativity in Macura's work. This symbiosis is pervasive in his tetralogy of historical prose fiction, *Ten, který bude* (He who will be, 1999), of which *Guvernantka* forms the third part. Conversely, however, Macura's scholarship is marked by a rare flair for cultural-meaning production, for how phenomena become symbolically charged and how they interconnect to shape a specific whole. It also reveals a well-developed sense of playfulness, mystifications, and games.

Macura was a literary historian by profession. Born in Ostrava in 1945 (his father was a metallurgical engineer), he moved to Prague in 1963 to study Czech and English at Charles University. From 1969, a year after graduation, he worked at the Institute of Czech Literature of the Czechoslovak Academy of Sciences. He was the institute's director from 1993 until his premature death from leukemia in 1999. Macura received solid training in the Czech structuralist tradition from the literary scholar Felix Vodička (1909–74), his professor and mentor at

Charles University, as well as a life-long interest in the Czech National Revival. Around 1970, Macura discovered what was to become another major source of inspiration—Yuri M. Lotman and the Tartu School of semiotics. Macura wrote extensively on Czech literature, especially poetry, from the early nineteenth century through the interwar avant-garde period and beyond, but his interest in semiotics gradually broadened his perspective and took his research in more interdisciplinary directions, toward cultural studies and history.[2]

Macura's preferred genre was the essay rather than the monograph, and most of these essays he gathered into four consistent volumes, all of which are represented here. His first major study and perhaps his academic magnum opus is his *Znamení zrodu* (Sign[s] of the birth, 1983), an analysis of "the Czech National Revival as a cultural type," as the subtitle fittingly defines his approach to the theme. It was methodologically pathbreaking and refreshingly unorthodox, and when the book came out, the one thousand copies that were printed sold out in a day.[3] In 1995 Macura therefore published a second edition to which he added two new chapters. With the collection *Český sen* (1998), he took his study of Czech myths and emblems deeper into the nineteenth century.

The democratic revolution of 1989 allowed him to publish his collection *Šťastný věk* (The joyous age, 1992), a penetrating analysis of the symbols, emblems, and myths of the Communist period. Macura also responded to the transformations following the Velvet Revolution with a series of brief semiotic essays, which he labeled *semi(o)fejetony* (semi[o]-sketches), small texts with a primarily contemporary focus, analyzing anything from national symbols, such as the nation's flag, its anthem, and the statesman Alexander Dubček, to even the arrival of McDonald's to Czechoslovakia. A collection of these essays appeared in 1993 as *Masarykovy boty* (Masaryk's boots).

At first, it may appear difficult to discern a common denominator among such varied studies as the semiotics of flower language during the National Revival, the Communist cult of the executed war hero Julius Fučík, or the symbolism of new Czech banknotes after the Velvet Divorce from the Slovaks 1992–93, but Macura reads all these phenomena as contributing to the constituting or reconstituting of a unique "Czech world" or culture. The following quotation may illuminate the trajectory of Macura's project:

> For its contemporary participant, the existence of Czech culture is self-evident. Czech culture surrounds him or her as a seemingly autonomous environment. It is a "whole" which is differentiated both socially and territorially. Composed of distinct parts, it is at the same time more or less "complete" and represents a

specifically "Czech world." Such a world is an example of what Yuri Lotman calls a "semiosphere."[4]

Macura's oeuvre can be read as an analysis of the interplay between the parts and the whole within this Czech semiosphere and more radically as an attempt to demonstrate how the modalities or even the very existence of a specific Czech culture were something far less self-evident than usually presumed.[5] Macura saw the National Revival as a kind of "big bang" in the formation of modern Czech high culture, and he constantly sought to demonstrate how the "signs of the birth"—that is, the norms, symbols, and cultural codes established in the Revival—continued to leave its mark on Czech culture even toward the end of the twentieth century. Macura further argued that this impact paradoxically asserted itself most intensively when the Czechs claimed to break most fundamentally with their national past, hence his fascination with moments of rupture and new beginnings, be it after the Communist seizure of power in 1948 or its collapse in 1989.

This anthology presents examples of Macura's work from all these periods. Part I covers the semiotics and cultural practices of the National Revival, while part II focuses on the emblems of Stalinism in Czechoslovakia of the 1950s and on the echoes of Czech mythologies audible even today. Before presenting each part in more detail, a few words of introduction may be needed in regard to the political and cultural situation of the Czechs at the beginning of the National Revival.

At the beginning of the nineteenth century, Bohemia and Moravia, the two core provinces or "Lands of the Bohemian Crown" that make up today's Czech Republic, formed an integral part of the Habsburg Empire. After the quenching of the rebellion of the Bohemian estates against the Habsburgs following the battle at the White Mountain outside Prague in 1620, the Czech language experienced a slow but steady decline as a medium of high culture—of administration, scholarship, art, and commerce—in Bohemia and Moravia. Around 1800, Czech remained the mother tongue of about two-thirds of the population, but all educated elites spoke German, and bilingualism in various forms and degrees was widespread.

At this time, Macura claims, Czech culture understood as a distinct, autonomous, more or less all-encompassing whole based on the Czech language, that is, a Czech *semiosphere*, seemed almost a contradiction in terms, because communication in Czech was restricted to a few limited functions within a larger cultural universe based on the German language. This situation presented the early Czech patriots of the so-called Jungmann generation (named after the scholar

Josef Jungmann, 1773–1847) with a choice: They could accept the status and role of Czech culture as a "culture within a culture" with restricted social foundations and limited social use and strive for its gradual expansion "from below," or they could present Czech culture as a fully developed, rich, and complex universe for a Czech national community equipped with and entitled to a role among the civilized nations of Europe. The patriots opted for the latter strategy, and Macura's *Znamení zrodu* can be said to represent an analysis of the consequences of this choice.

In so doing, the Czech patriots were clearly inspired by general trends in Europe, and their national cultural model was characterized by extensive borrowings, especially from German national Romanticism. Under these special Czech circumstances, however, these transplantations often—even when preserving a superficial similarity to their prototypes—acquired altogether new functions and meanings. To begin with, the chosen strategy had one paradoxical consequence: In simulating an entire, organic Czech high culture, the patriots actually ruptured the social roots of the existing cultural production in the Czech language, which served different purposes and expressed very different messages. Macura has shown how these mechanisms affected the period's Czech theater (Václav Klicpera, Jan Nepomuk Štěpánek), which could not be integrated into the Jungmann generation's high-flown model of a national culture because it had to cater to the needs of a real audience in order to sell tickets. The cultural distance between the patriotic elites and the vast majority of the Czech-speaking population thus increased dramatically, and without a social *hinterland*, the patriotic project assumed a highly artificial character: Czech high culture in this version existed almost exclusively in and as *texts*, providing, in Macura's words, "an extremely strong semiotization of any constitutive element of the Czech world."[6] Although not explicit about this, Macura seems to have considered this situation historically *unique*: In the early nineteenth century, following the French Revolution's shattering of the old social cosmology and before the consolidation of the nationally defined semiospheres into which we are born today, a rare window of opportunity existed for creativity and *choice* with regard to national identity. New national worlds could be discursively created in ways impossible later on.

This special situation invites two research strategies: One is to study the microhistory of this creative "patriotic community," the particular personal contacts and relations characterizing it and affecting its cultural activities, the prevailing approach in *Český sen* (and also, one feels tempted to argue, in *Ten, který bude*). Or one can employ a structural approach, focusing on this culture as a system, as done in *Znamení zrodu*, which Macura consequently divided in two parts, enlarged in the second edition with a third section, *Paradoxy*, containing the previously mentioned discussion of Czech theater. He devoted the first section to the constitutive features of this "cultural type"—its morphology (*tvarosloví*) in Macura's slightly idiosyncratic terms—and the second one to some of its key terms or concepts (*pojmosloví*). The essays "The Center" and "Prague" in the first part of this book are examples of Macura's analysis of such key concepts.

At the very core of the revival culture was its *lingua-centrism*, that is, its extreme focus on the Czech language, leading at times to its sacralization. This emphasis was necessary, because the Czech language was the *only* effective marker of Czech nationality in early nineteenth-century Bohemia. And with the given shape of this language, its cultivation—and innovation in terms of vocabulary—became a precondition for consolidating a national community. So in a demiurgic act of naming, an entire Czech world was virtually spoken into being, which for decades existed in the sphere of language alone, a language that in its inventiveness and artificiality was nearly incomprehensible for the uninitiated. A novel in Czech simulated the existence of a Czech literary public, and Czech scientific terminology feigned the existence of a Czech intellectual elite, and both types of texts were produced to serve the language rather than vice versa. As Jungmann put it: "The language is in need of cultivation, which is achieved by the cultivation of sciences."[7]

This inverted order, where criteria of content (truthfulness, relevance) were subordinated to aesthetic and ideological norms, made *syncretism* a main feature of the Revivalist culture. There was a very poor differentiation of genres; all writing was directed toward the goal of developing a Czech national culture. Nor was there a normal hierarchy between central and peripheral cultural manifestations, as Macura wittily demonstrates with the language of flowers, which received unusual ideological attention; the rose and the lily symbolize the national colors, the linden tree represents Slavdom, and so on. The entire Revivalist project was interpreted in horticultural metaphors of the cultivation of the national garden, which appeared as a closed microcosm, a mythical Eden. As shown in the chapter "Where Is My Home?" the text of the Czech national anthem abounds with such images.

Borrowing from more well-developed high cultures was, as mentioned, pivotal in this process, and *translation* ("the transplanting of foreign flowers" in the contemporary parlance) was of special importance. From a communicative perspective, these translations were mostly dysfunctional: texts in German, in particular, were translated from a language every educated reader in Bohemia understood into a language used by virtually no one at that level. However, the goal was not to introduce some textual information to a new readership, but to demonstrate that this information could be expressed in Czech as well. Hence, great attention was paid to the translator, whose name figured prominently on the title page, and who was entitled to great liberties in adapting or at times rewriting (as in the Czech appropriation of Johann Gottfried von Herder) the content to make it suit the norms and needs of the "Revivalist project."

The overriding ambition of the patriots was to emancipate this Czech world from omnipresent German culture while also demonstrating that Czech culture was just as rich, varied, and prestigious as the German rival. In all spheres, the juxtaposition of Czech (or Slav) and German was therefore obligatory: Czech verse had to use "non-German" meters, Czech philology had to provide evidence of the profound differences between the two languages (or, only seemingly in contradiction to this, demonstrate how Czech had degenerated through German influence, from which it had to be cleansed to retrieve its Slavic purity). In a twofold sense, the *mirroring* of German examples thus became a cardinal structural characteristic of the Czech revival: by *negation* (to prove the peculiarity of the Czechs) and by *copying* (to prove the competitiveness of the Czechs at all levels, culturally as well as institutionally). This "negative and analogue tie" remained strong long after the "high Revival" and testifies to the continued dependency of German culture long into the nineteenth century. The essay "Dream of Europe" shows how a similar ambiguity characterized the Czech approach to Europe. The Czech elites longed to be seen and recognized both as unmistakably European and as something special, a unique nation among the many peoples of Europe. Macura takes his analysis all the way to the Central Europe debates of the 1980s and makes due reference to the key role of the motif of the center in these discourses, which is also analyzed in the chapter "The Center."

Historical references played a vital role in the Revivalist project, but unlike in the historical criticism of the Enlightenment, their use was subordinated in every respect to the needs of national ideology. As the very term "revival" suggests, the creation of a modern Czech nation was often portrayed as the "rebirth" or "resurrection" of the national body after a long slumber, and in line with this image, the past was presented as an essentially timeless, mythical tale, giving evidence of what was to come. Thus, if in accordance with general European trends (and in order to mirror German culture) an "original" medieval culture was called for, it had to be created. Hence the discovery in 1817 and 1818 of two early medieval manuscripts, the Královédvorský (Queen's Court) and Zelenohorský (Green Mountain) manuscripts, written in what appeared to be old Czech. The manuscripts created a sensation among patriotic circles and contributed tremendously (and along with them Václav Hanka [1791–1861], their primary author) to the consolidation of the national community. In portraying a Czech past that was at least as rich and venerable as the German, they bolstered national pride and "proved" the legitimacy of contemporary Czech claims to equality with the Germans.

The eminent philologist Josef Dobrovský (1753–1829) dismissed the manuscripts as forgeries, but his criticism was repudiated by Jungmann and his followers as proof of its author's "hyper-criticism" and lack of patriotism. According to Macura, later Czech interpretations have explained Hanka's forgeries and Jungmann's attack on Dobrovský as exceptional flaws in the two men's characters, something not typical for the Revival as a whole, but in reality, mystifications like these were quite common and acceptable in the Revivalist culture, as they generally were throughout European Romanticism. In the Czech case, however, Macura argues, this trait attained unusual proportions because all of Czech contemporary culture looked more fictional than real and therefore not bound by the rules of the material world.[8] As the poet Ján Kollár (1793–1852) put it: "We are playing a piano, which still, it seems, has no strings in it."[9] Elements of "game playing" were therefore extraordinarily common in the Revivalist culture, and the essay "Mystification and the Nation" reveals how Hanka's forgeries were an integral part of this game. In the 1820s patriots even composed parodies of the manuscripts, thus it makes little sense to draw any sharp distinction between joke and forgery in the Revivalist culture. Later, as Czech high culture began to address a real audience and function in a real social context, communicative truthfulness inevitably became a primary value.

The "coming out" of the textual ghetto was a prolonged process, and early public demonstrations of Czech patriotism (the use of Czech greetings, the arranging of Czech balls where only Czech was spoken, and so on) appeared highly artificial. To outsiders, the patriotic community looked like a sect or a secret society, and Macura has demonstrated how this society had rituals typical of sects, whether it was in the talk of "initiation" as a patriot or in the adding of an invented patriotic middle name to one's given name. Macura often points to changes in the meaning and use of key concepts and symbols, but generally speaking, the processes that transformed a closed, introverted, textually oriented cultural production into a normally functioning national cultural life remains underexplained in his work, especially in the structuralist studies of *Znamení zrodu*. Macura was most at home when analyzing highly ideologically charged and relatively static semiotic systems, which made it natural for him to analyze the Communist era and in particular its Stalinist beginnings.

With the Communist seizure of power in 1948, Czechoslovak society was immediately forced to adopt and reproduce Soviet procedures and models at all levels. High Stalinism offered a fully developed cultural model where every phenomenon was allocated a specific, often highly emblematic role and function in a strongly utopian narrative, an eschatological vision of the installment of paradise on earth after the final battle between good and evil.[10] A key point in Macura's readings of how this imported cultural model attained Czech features is the observation that it shared many key structuring features with the cultural model of the National Revival, and that this affinity facilitated the adaptation of Czech culture to Stalinist paradigms.[11] The ample use of Hussite references and symbols in connection with the death and burial of the Communist leader Klement Gottwald (1896–1953), described in the essay "Death of the Leader," testifies to this. The contrast to the equally intense, but multifarious, semiotization of former Party leader Alexander Dubček at the time of his death in 1992, analyzed in the essay "Symbol with a Human Face," is striking.

Parallels to the Revivalist model are also revealed in Macura's essay on how the cult of I. V. Michurin (1855–1935), a Russian fruit grower, was imported to Czechoslovakia. The notion of a paradise on earth, which already *is* a reality (in the form of the Soviet Union), but which also must be cultivated (an image stressing the organic, natural dimensions of the building of socialism), resonated well with similar Revivalist motifs of the Czech motherland as a mythical garden, an Eden safely set aside from the storms of the world of historicity. Threats to this garden had to come from outside, in the form of foreign vermin seeking to penetrate and destroy the fruits of joyous labor in this paradise or from what remained of domestic snakes from the period before the creation of Eden. In "The Potato Bug," Macura wittily demonstrates how the Colorado beetle was promoted as a key symbol in the struggle against foreign imperialists and internal enemies around 1950, a case that shows again how hierarchies of what was central and what was peripheral in a cultural system could attain highly unusual forms when a seemingly marginal phenomenon was endowed with emblematic status.

The "Spartakiad," an enormous national gymnastics festival organized by the Communists beginning in 1955, is an example of how the regime dealt with an inherited national institution. The so-called Sokol (Falcon) gymnastics movement, founded in 1862 (after German paradigms) by Miroslav Tyrš (1832–84) and Jindřich Fügner (1822–65), soon became a significant vehicle for national mobilization, and its gymnastic festivals, eleven of which were organized between 1882 and 1848, enjoyed massive popular support.[12] The adaptation of this "bourgeois-nationalist" heritage had to be more troublesome than the recodification of older historical symbols such as the Hussites, because thousands of Czechs had living memories of their time as Sokol members, associating it with the "old regime." Macura's essay on Spartakiad offers a careful analysis of those aspects of Sokol that could be recycled, and what had to be added, and of how the phenomenon of mass gymnastics could be transformed into a showcase demonstration of Socialist norms and values.

In the mid-1950s it was still possible to orchestrate Spartakiad as a coherent symbol of the virtues of Socialism. But as shown in "The Metro," Macura's analysis of the building of Prague's metro, the production of a similarly coherent semantic gesture was far more difficult twenty years later. The metro was the primary Socialist prestige project of the 1970s and 1980s, and much was done to make it appear as a symbol of Czechoslovak–Soviet friendship and cooperation and as a spectacular manifestation of the advanced skills of a mature Socialist society. But the prosaic functions of the metro itself and the "insufficient possibilities for its patheticization" ("The Metro") after the crumbling of the cultural model of high Stalinism since the late 1950s severely limited the metro's emblematic power. A century of constant technological innovation had also contributed to trivializing such endeavors, as the comparison of the response to the first trains among Czech poets in the mid-nineteenth century to the reception of the metro illustrates. Instead, contemporary Czech poetry turned to more general, nonideological images and metaphors associated with the metro's underground location, motifs that corresponded badly with the official rhetoric surrounding the project.

The fall of Communism in 1989 also brought the collapse of what remained of Stalinism as a cultural type, but as the small "semi(o)-sketch" "Minus-Stalin" demonstrates, the resulting emptiness was not neutral. Anything brought in to fill the void inevitably commented on it, be it as an involuntary echoing of its practices (as Macura points out in "Renaming," an essay regarding the frequent renaming of streets and other public places after 1989) or with more subtle, subversive gestures, as in the case of the metronome at the location of the old Stalin monument. Under Macura's gaze, the Czechs seem to be subjecting even the most prosaic phenomena to semiotization. As we see in the short essay "The Celts within Us," even a Czech cookbook from 1992 can thus become the starting point for an analysis of how and why the first known inhabitants of Bohemia, the ancient Celts, can again become a mirror for Czech self-definition. The window of opportunity for creating new worlds may no longer be as big as during the National Revival, but Macura's Czechs live in a very long nineteenth century, and as Macura ironically concludes, "to doubt [their creativity] would surely be foolish."

In the mid-1980s, when the straitjacket of Marxist-Leninist orthodoxy still placed severe limits on what Czech scholars could openly discuss and do, Macura coedited *Průvodce po světové literární teorii* (Guide to world literary theory, 1988). Using the format of the encyclopedia, the handbook presented eighty books by eighty literary scholars in the broadest sense, from Beda Allemann and Erich Auerbach to William Wimsatt and V. M. Zhirmunsky. This format allowed for an introduction to neglected or denounced theories and approaches. Here Macura wrote about Lotman, but another entry of his was devoted to Johan Huizinga's *Homo ludens* (Playing man).[13] Macura clearly sensed a deep affinity with Huizinga's theories about the importance and creative potential of the "play-element" in human culture,[14] and a "serious playfulness" pervades his entire oeuvre, both as a research strategy and as a method of writing. This strategy was arguably as analytically fruitful as it was aesthetically pleasing, and the historian Jaroslav Marek's complaint in his review of *Masarykovy boty* that Macura showed an "ironic lack of respect" for, and a "stubborn devaluation of everything that anyone could perhaps still consider high and noble in the past"[15] seems a complete misunderstanding of Macura's intentions.

Macura's sympathy for the actors of the National Revival is evident, as is his fascination with its culture. Macura was afraid to use a quotation from Antonín Marek (1785–1877) as a motto to the first edition of *Znamení zrodu*, because it all too clearly pointed to the semiotic nature of the study. But the motto found its way into the second edition, and in *Český sen*, Macura's last book published in his lifetime, the final chapter, *Sen o semiotice* (The dream of semiotics), is devoted to Marek. Macura demonstrates how Marek's book of 1820, *Logika nebo umnice* (Logic, or reasoning), the source of the quotation, was actually a translation from German, and how it represented an example of the Czech attempt to create scientific terminology for the future. Toward the end of the chapter, Macura dwells on what Marek saw as the use of semiotics. It was, he held, a science that "teaches either how to invent beautiful signs, or to find one's way in signs of beautiful meaning."[16] This came close to a credo for Macura, for whom semiotic studies in his own words, echoing Marek, remained "a playful art with the help of which we invent suitable signs, or find those meanings that suit us."[17]

Macura himself preserved this playfulness to the very end. If we look at his last novel, *Medikus* (The physician), published posthumously in 1999, we see that the final word in the last sentence is *znamení* (sign)!

PART I

The Nineteenth Century
Genesis of a Nation

1

Where Is My Home?

The song "Kde domov můj" (Where Is My Home?) was written by the Czech drama-
tist Josef Kajetán Tyl and the composer František Škroup for the dramatic comedy
Fidlovačka (Spring Folk Festival), first performed in 1834. The song quickly became
popular among the Czechs, and after the founding of Czechoslovakia in 1918, it
became the first part of the country's national anthem.

Kde domov můj, kde domov můj?
Voda hučí po lučinách,
Bory šumí po skalinách,
V sadě skví se jara květ,
Zemský ráj to na pohled!
A to je ta krásná země,
Země česká, domov můj,
Země česká, domov můj!

Kde domov můj, kde domov můj?
V kraji znáš-li bohumilém
Duše útlé v těle čilém,
Mysl jasnou, vznik a zdar,
A tu sílu vzdoru zmar!
To je Čechů slavné plémě,
Mezi Čechy domov můj,
Mezi Čechy domov můj.

[Where is my home, where is my home?
Water roars across the meadows,
Pinewoods rustle among the crags,
The garden is glorious with spring blossom,
Paradise on earth it is to see.

3

And this is that beautiful land,
The Czech land, my home,
The Czech land, my home.

Where is my home, where is my home?
If, in a heavenly land, you have met
Tender souls in agile frames,
Of clear mind, vigorous and prospering,
And with a strength that frustrates all defiance,
That is the glorious race of Czechs,
Among the Czechs is my home,
Among the Czechs is my home.]

"My native land, my joy, my home," sing the Estonians. The Latvians entrust their country to God's protection. Other hymns ask for a ruler's protection. "Unbreakable union of freeborn republics great Russia has welded forever to stand," maintains the anthem of the former Soviet Union in a tone that brooks no reservation. "Arise children of the fatherland, the day of glory has arrived," aggressively summons the Marseillaise. The Czech national anthem opens with a question, "Where is my home?"

This opening has already been the subject of considerable deliberation, and analogies have been sought both locally and abroad. A similar conceit appears in František Turinský's *Angelína:** "Where is my country? / Where the oak tops tower? / Where the eagle flies toward the sun? / Where the thickly leaved linden cools, / the slender pine trembles on the cliff? / That is my country!" The Czech anthem also recalls Ján Kollár[†] ("Do you know this land, this country of the eternal Sláva, the paradise of all loveliness"), as well as Mignon's famous song in Johann Wolfgang von Goethe's 1795–96 work Wilhelm Meisters Lehrjahre (*Wilhelm Meister's* Apprenticeship) ("Kennst du das Land, wo die Zitronen blühen") (Do you know the land where the lemons blossom). Yet one way or another, these affinities and analogies, while appearing to assert the typicality of this poetic introductory query and its popularity at the time, rather confirm our

---

* František Turinský (1797–1852) was a Czech poet and dramatist. His tragedy *Angelína* (1821) is his best-known work.

† Ján Kollár (1793–1852) was a Slovak poet, prose writer, and Pan-Slavist. His most famous work, *Sláva dcery* (Daughter of Sláva, 1824), a cycle of Petrarchan sonnets glorifying the history of the Slavs and lamenting their present state, made him famous throughout the Slavic world.

suspicions. After all, Angelína is speaking about a far-away country and recalls it from distant shores as if it were something unreal, virtually impossible. Mignon also sings of an unattainable country hidden somewhere beyond the horizon. And Kollár's verse concerns an unreal supernatural country, not at all resembling a land on which mortals tread.

The anthem's interrogatory opening concerning the whereabouts of the Czech homeland betrays uncertainty, a lack of self-evidence, and a sense of the homeland's unattainability. Moreover, the scene for which the song was written is revealing: It is a blind man who inquires as to the existence of the homeland. As is well-known, the song was written to herald the appearance of the blind fiddler Mareš in Josef Kajetán Tyl's farce *Fidlovačka*.* To be sure, an answer follows shortly. With his song, the unseeing old man creates an imaginary representation of the "Czech land" with "purling water," "rustling pines," and "spring in flower." But this image is too vague, general, and symbolic to provide reassurance. The country set forth in the answer is merely an ideal paradisiacal country that will never be glimpsed, not only because it is a blind man who creates it in his imagination, but because a blind man speaks about a "paradise visible."

The history of the song is awash with attempts to anchor it in a concrete country. Dozens of pastiches have been created trying to provide it with the most familiar and cherished content. Minor changes have allowed it to be sung as a Moravian song ("Moravian land—my homeland"), a Silesian song ("Silesian land—my homeland"), and as a song of almost any region: "pod Radhoštem, my homeland," "in Jaroměř, my homeland," "Glorious Mělník, my homeland," "Kutná hora, my homeland," "city of Náchod, my homeland." But none of these attempts to make the images of the homeland more intimate has succeeded in establishing the homeland as a self-evident certainty or an unproblematic fact.

The homeland as a natural geographic and historical region in the life of a national community (a community that during the revival of Czech culture seemed alienated from the present, relegated to the realm of sheer idealism) competed in the nineteenth century with another homeland—an abstract, fabricated region of cultural, primarily literary, values. It is worth noting how often Czech literature is spoken of precisely in this metaphorical cliché. In the once widely read almanac *Lada Nióla* (1855),† F. L. Vorlíček contrasted the barren

---

* Josef Kajetán Tyl (1808–56) was a dramatist and prose writer. *Fidlovačka* (Spring Folk Festival) was first performed in 1834 and is the source of the Czech national anthem "Where Is My Home?"

† While not as famous or influential as Jan Neruda's almanac *Máj* (1858), J. V. Frič's *Lada Nióla* presented and debated questions of Czech national identity.

landscape of "pre Revivalist" Czech literature ("a dry riverbed," "once fruitful meadows have become clogged with rum and rocks," "the grapevines seem to have been choked at the roots," "meadows and gardens of beauty, stands of heavenly poetry, have been covered by time's deluge of deleterious ice floes") with the "beauteous landscape" of the emerging Czech literature: "A mighty current hurtling forward, bordered with a bright-hued carpet of flowering meadows; somewhat higher I see quivering in the soft breeze the auspicious harvest, interwoven with assiduously guarded orchards and vineyards, vineyards which, resting against hillocks overgrown with the wild green of bushes and breaking up the broad plateau, offer the eye, immersed in all this beauty, a lengthy rest. From the other side wondrous gardens emerge before my eyes, boasting flowers of mellifluous colors, numerous paths, fountains, lush bowers, and shadowy groves filled with entire flocks of songbirds and summoning my soul with the same seductive allure. To tarry a moment and imbibe their magical impressions."

Karolína Světlá* describes the development of Czech letters along the same lines: "Snowdrops, violets, lilies spring up to adorn the ravaged leas, and up above, delightful shrubbery entwine their young verdant branches. *Hvĕvkovský, Puchmajer, Kramerius, Kamarýt,*† and their contemporaries appeared on the orphaned field of Czech letters. "The hillside covered with "thyme," "lilies," and "dark carnations" is Erben† to her. The nightingale awakening the "cabbage rose" represents František Ladislav Čelakovský§; in the "pine grove" purple raspberries ripen "on a thorny stick." And František Jaromír "Rubeš**" and his companions distributed his refreshing fruits swishing mischievously their prickly stick of humor. "Here is a "fount" spreading out in a "crystal current." "Tyl dipped his pen into his own heart, and the nation resounded with all the love issuing therefrom." "A lake in the mists" is Karel Hynek Mácha.†† Among the

---

* Karolína Světlá (1830–99) was a Romantic Czech novelist and feminist.
† Šebestian Hvĕvkovský (1770–1874) was a burlesque poet. Antonín Puchmajer (1769–1820) was known as a poet, priest, and philologist. Václav Matěj Kramerius (1753–1808) was a journalist, publisher, and translator. Josef Vlastimil Kamarýt (1797–1833) was a poet.
† Karel Jaromír Erben (1811–70) was a folktale collector, ethnographer, and poet. His collection of ballads in the spirit of Goethe and Gottfried August Bürger, *A Bouquet of National Tales* (1853), is a national classic.
§ František Ladislav Čelakovský (1799–1852) was a Czech folklorist and poet. Beginning in 1822, he collected Slavic folk songs, which he later imitated in his own books of verse, *Echoes of Russian Song* (1829) and *Echoes of Czech Song* (1839).
** František Jaromír Rubeš (1814–53) was a humorist.
†† Karel Hynek Mácha (1810–36) was the first (and only) Czech Romantic poet. *May* (1836) is his greatest work.

smaller ornaments of this allegorical garden belong the "golden fortress," symbolizing Josef Jungmann* and his dictionary. Next to him is the "linden tree," representing Pavel Josef Šafařík.† Above him the "eagle" Kollár rises awakening the nation from the grave with his wings, and so on.

The symbolic language used here to address literary matters differs profoundly from the language we use to describe literary material today. At the same time, it is surprising how much the "landscape of the anthem" resembles this "landscape of literature"—yet with one fundamental exception: The landscape of literature is a landscape of certainty; it was precisely this landscape that in the nineteenth century was "given in inheritance" to the nation, "this broad land, one of a kind land." This landscape was not wistful longing for the unrealizable. It was the only self-evident Czech world.

The anthem was a song of vain yearning and pining. Stories circulated about the song, for example, about how the English queen was reduced to tears, how it emotionally touched Czechs living abroad. Literature—that was the homeland they didn't have to share, the homeland that belonged to them alone, and for which they did not have to pine. It was a homeland they had created for themselves, a homeland that simply and plainly was.

* Josef Jungmann (1773–1847) was a linguist, poet, and translator. He systematically adapted words from other Slavic languages to Czech. He also translated several works of world literature into the new Czech literary language.
† Pavel Josef Šafařík (1795–1861) was a historian and philologist.

2

Mystification and the Nation

Following the Battle of White Mountain in 1620, the Czech lands underwent a process of Germanization due to the policies of the Habsburg emperors. The Czech language was abolished from state administration, journalism, schools, and literature and was reduced to the language of the peasantry, cooks, and stable hands. During the eighteenth and nineteenth centuries, the Czechs underwent a National Revival, a cultural movement to revive the Czech language, culture, and national identity. The most prominent figures of the National Revival were Josef Dobrovský, Josef Jungmann, and Pavel Jozef Šafařík.

Mystification faithfully accompanied the first manifestations of the Czech Revivalist intelligentsia's attempts at emancipation. In 1816 Josef Linda "discovered" the Song of Vyšehrad, which happened to be in the binding of a book he owned. A year later in the town of Dvůr Králové nad Labem, Václav Hanka "discovered" part of a rich anthology of Czech poetry from the Middle Ages, which utterly transformed the previous conception of old Czech literature. In 1818 an anonymous manuscript, the Zelenohorský manuscript, made its way to the table of the supreme Czech burgrave Count Kolovrat Libštejnský, purported to be a literary document from the ninth century.* Later, several Czech songs by King Václav† were discovered in a museum, which relegated the German versions to mere translations from the Czech. As if by chance, on the reverse side of this document was an older version of the song "Jelen" (Stag) from the Královédvorský manuscript. Thereon followed the discovery of a Czech commentary inside the *Mater Verborum*,‡ the

---

* The manuscripts of "Dvůr Králové" (Královédvorský) and "Zelená Hora" (Zelenohorský) are epic Slavic manuscripts "discovered" by Václav Hanka and Josef Kovář, respectively. Later they were determined to be forgeries produced by Hanka and his friend Josef Linda. Many Czech nationalists insisted they were genuine.

† King Václav I (907–29) is allegedly the author of three surviving German love poems.

‡ The *Mater Verborum* is a genuine Czech encyclopedia from the first half of the thirteenth century. It is one of the finest examples of Romanesque illumination.

discovery of an interlinear translation of the Gospel according to John, forgeries of hymns in the psalter in the National Gallery, counterfeit coins bearing a Slavic inscription, and so on.

But these are not cases of classic literary forgeries. The beginning of the nineteenth century was simply a period unusually inclined to mystificatory behavior. Like a bolt from the blue, a mature Czech poetess by the name of Žofie Jandová appeared on the scene, but it soon came to light that her work was a forgery by František Ladislav Čelakovský.* This, however, did not prevent Čelakovský from smuggling the unmasked sham poetess into a representative collection of translated Czech poetry, John Bowring's *Cheskian Anthology* (1832). Mystificatory high jinks accompanied the publication of *The Foundations of Czech Poetry*,† Ján Kollár included fake songs in his *National Songs*, Václav Hanka forged a Moravian anthem for the Moravians, and Franz Liszt was hoodwinked by a false Hussite song.‡ Čelakovský's preserved correspondence is full of various mystificatory jokes as well.

The main point here, however, is not the amount of recorded forgeries but, rather, something much more fundamental. Jungmann's decision in favor of "Czech culture" as a complete and entire structure with all the appropriate appurtenances—Czech physics, chemistry, mathematics, military science, aesthetics, philosophy, and so on—was perforce far ahead of immediate needs. Specialized terminology was created along with specialized texts and exclusive poetic works, even though no social class existed that would make use of them. In other words, this meant that specialized Czech studies, classical tragedies, and so on necessarily created the illusion that a culturally developed Czech society existed with significant scientific and aesthetic strata, along with a refined and somewhat conservative taste, which cultivated these genres. Revivalist culture mystified (and could not but mystify) as a whole. It feigned for itself and the rest of the world the self-evidence of its existence. Seen in this context, it is clear that mystification was not anything unusual. It was not an anomaly or a small island of incidental deception in an otherwise authentic sea of Czech culture.

* František Ladislav Čelakovský (1799–1852) was a Czech folklorist and poet. Beginning in 1822 he collected Slavic folk songs, which he later imitated in his own books of verse, *Echoes of Russian Song* (1829) and *Echoes of Czech Song* (1839).
† Published in 1818 by František Palacký and Pavel Šafařík, *The Foundations of Czech Poetry* was a defense of quantitative verse in Czech poetry and an attack on the authority of the great Revivalist Josef Dobrovský.
‡ The Hungarian composer Franz Liszt (1811–86) was given a Czech drinking song and told it was a Hussite hymn. The tune subsequently made its way throughout Europe in Liszt's version.

Just as a work written in Czech on experimental psychology constructed—of course only by way of hints—a partial segment of the cultural organism in the present, the forgeries of ancient literary monuments put the finishing touches on the "past" of this selfsame cultural organism. It was necessary to create an entire Czech culture as quickly as possible, which in turn necessitated the simultaneous creation of its supplementary "traditions," which would better correspond to the magnificent Revivalist dream.

At the same time, the border between seriousness and fraud was just about as clear as the border between a game and a joke. Shortly after the discovery of the Zelenohorský and Královédvorský manuscripts, Josef Linda, who along with Hanka is one of the prime suspects in the manuscript controversy, published in a journal he edited a poem titled "Volmír, A New Antique," in which he clearly ironized the style and language of a discovery that was meant to be a sacred monument. To read something like this today—moreover from Linda—is as if to glimpse a sly wink from the distant past. And when, with Hanka's assistance, the German scholar Eberhard Gottlieb Graff discovered marginal Czech notes in the Latin dictionary *Mater Verborum*, among which one finds the shocking translation of the word "German" as "barbarus, tardus, truculentus," what are we to make of this? Is it a malicious, crude hoax perpetrated by "Czech nationalists" or merely a joke?

The histrionic dreams of a glorious Czech past and glorious Czech future were also often accompanied by a self-ironic suspicion of the futility of this grand and considerably artificial task that the Revivalists had set themselves. We witness this bipolarity from the very beginning—glorifications of Czech grandeur along with expressions of skepticism, usually in private unpublished texts. At times they are almost tragic in their solemnity; other times they relax and let off steam by joking and parodying themselves. This other, skeptical pole is life giving and therapeutic. It is doubtlessly due primarily to this pole that Czech culture managed to free itself relatively quickly from the artificial character of much of the Revival.

Nevertheless, the "Zelenohorský" and "Královédvorský" forgeries influenced Czech culture for some time. They created "great themes" for literature, visual art, and music. They became artistic sources and impulses comparable to the ancient tradition or the Bible. Thus, ultimately, it was difficult to reject and discredit them as a "lie," for they had become too integral to the fabric of Czech culture. In the second half of the nineteenth century, a normally functioning culture of an existent, socially stratified, even "modern," if somewhat neurotic, national community stood on a long-standing lie. The battle against the manuscripts once again struck at the very roots of national existence.

Thus, mystification played a different, more significant role than elsewhere in Europe. Playfulness was certainly involved, but its primary functions were decidedly not those of a game nor were they the project of a new aesthetic. Czech mystification always bore culturally and nationally creative aspects within it that were supposed to provide evidence of the remarkable values of the Czech nation. They were meant to serve as proof of its ancient heritage, as testimony to glorious deeds of the past and the high level of its cultural development. This mystification, of course, based Czech national identity on a fiction, so much so in fact that the doubting of the forgeries became *the* sign of genuine national emancipation. The rejection of the manuscripts was actually a continuation of the aforementioned overall "self-ironic gesture." The gesture, which at first created at most only a secondary subtext of Revivalist euphoria—one that was easily downplayed—was continued in the demythologizing analyses of the manuscripts' opponents, specifically in the literary works of Karel Havlíček and Jan Neruda.

Sometimes it seems as if the mystification of the nineteenth century led directly to the mystifications and the mystificatory games of the present, that is, to the monumental joke of the Czech polyhistorian Jára da Cimrman* to Jarmil Křemen† to the mystification of a film about the November Revolution,‡ which began in 1990 in the magazine *Reflex*, to the staged visit of Woody Allen to Northern Bohemia,§ and so on.

Mystification that aspires to become a sacrosanct value is, however, in a way an abnormality. Only the abnormal conditions in which Czech culture found itself at the beginning of the nineteenth century could justify it. The real purpose of mystification is rather to demystify, and current mystificatory games bear this out.

---

* Jára da Cimrman is a Czech fictional character created by Jiří Šebánek, Zdeněk Svěrák, and Ladislav Smoljak in 1966. Originally he was a caricature of the Czech people, Czech history, Czech mythology, and Czech culture. The Jára Cimrman Theater in Žižkov, a section of Prague, is one of the most popular theaters in the Czech Republic. In a 2005 poll taken by Czech Television, Cimrman was voted the "Greatest Czech of All Time," but the organizers of the poll disqualified Cimrman on the grounds of his nonexistence.

† Jarmil Křemen is a fictional Czech literary historian invented by Macura around 1990.

‡ In 1993 Petr Zelenka directed a fictional feature-length documentary, *Visící zámek*, which chronicled the story of a fictional punk rock band and their instigation of the Velvet Revolution.

§ In 1993 Josef Formánek, the founder of the Czech magazine *Koktejl*, staged with Petr Poledňák a false visit by Woody Allen to Northern Bohemia, starring Radek John as Allen. The visit was reported by several leading Czech newspapers, and *The Guardian* considered "Woodygate" to be the best practical joke ever perpetrated by the Czechs.

Undoubtedly, this seems somewhat far-fetched, but the element in which mystification is at home is actually the agitation of ossified forms, be they literary or cultural, that is, their constant parody. The best example is the mystificatory game of Jára da Cimrman, which a large part of the population, along with the "foremost Cimrmanologists," has been playing for a number of years.

It is bizarre, to say the least, that there exists a theater bearing the name of this "Czech giant," that films and books devoted to him have been made, that an entire "culture" has arisen (one wants to say, "Just like during the National Revival") from this collective game. Moreover, if Smoljak and Svěrák succeed in renaming their current venue, the T. G. Masaryk Theater, the Theater of T. G. Masaryk and his Friend Cimrman, this would be a signal that our nation has truly come of age and has definitively thrown off its Revivalist swaddling clothes. It would signal the decisive victory of "self-irony" as well as the victory of the game that was present as a subtext of the "Revival mystification" over the false solemnity of a sacred task.

3

Dream of Europe

Throughout their history, the Czechs have seen themselves as, variously, standing at the center of Europe, at the edge of Europe, or as forming a bridge between the "civilized" West and the "barbaric" East. At times, they have cast themselves as the possessors of European values in their purest, most authentic form and, at other times, as the culture that can renew moribund Western civilization with an influx of Slavic values.

When the Pentecostal Uprising* broke out in Prague in 1848, Václav Vladivoj Tomek[†] was taking a walk through the city and witnessed an arresting scene: "In Alley Street, I saw the first barricade go up. As I continued toward Fruit Street, I saw a young man and two women on Franciscan Square. He began breaking up paving stones with an axe, obviously intending to erect another barricade. The frightened women were trying to restrain him, however, and just as I was walking by he shouted: 'Leave me alone, all of Europe is watching us.'"[1] At the time, this declaration was not characteristically Czech. It could be heard from Berlin to Frankfurt and all the way to Vienna, and it would return time and again during momentous periods. Tomek, who noted the event as a bizarre peculiarity, was evidently rather shocked by the fact that these words had made their way as far as Prague, as did the barricades and other attributes of revolution. But with this catch phrase, the man in the street, albeit indirectly, was referring to Europe as the relevant context for Czech affairs: for him Europe was the normative horizon for behavior and action. With a little imagination, we can visualize this man in the street at a later time and in a different place. He stands among a rather small crowd that has gathered in 1910 at a former vineyard tower on Vítkov Hill at the unveiling of a memorial plaque celebrating the ancient victory

---

* The Pentecostal Uprising took place in Prague from 12 to 17 June. It was the culmination of the 1848–49 revolutions in Bohemia.
† Václav Vladivoj Tomek (1818–1905) was a Czech historian and politician. His chief work is the twelve-volume *History of the City of Prague* (1855–1901).

of the Hussites: "Convinced of the rightness of their cause, a small number of people defeated the united ranks of armored fighters. At that time there were two sides—Europe and us. And Europe was pale and wan."

Two opposing pronouncements defined the two extreme poles of the Czech mindset vis-à-vis Europe. On one side stands the slogan of the nineteenth-century European revolutions. The Slovak Gustáv Kazimír Zechenter-Laskomerský heard it on every corner in Vienna ("The pitiful statements, again and again so profusely repeated: *Meine Herren! Europa schaut auf Euch!**).[2] The repetition of the exclamation in Prague was obviously meant to suggest that the Czech lands belonged on the same historical stage with Europe. European problems are their problems, thus Europeanism did not appear as something external and distinct. Czech nationalists sought it out as a matter of course even in areas that were traditionally considered reservoirs of Czechness. Of course, even the national Czech emancipation process (which was from the perspective of the opposition often seen as a superfluous, irrational movement whose consequences would irreparably disrupt European cultural ties) was in those days readily explained as a justifiable Pan-European affair ("We may boldly call our century the century of national awakening. . . . This powerful sentiment is convulsing all of Europe"[3]), whereby the Czech lands were merely paying their dues according to the general laws of cultural progress. From this perspective, the Czech world becomes a significant historical agent, declaring itself repeatedly as the very vanguard of European events. Once again we encounter a reference to the Hussite legacy, but this time for once it is "pro-European." It is perceived as foreshadowing the aspirations of the French revolutionaries. Such pronouncements were very common, and the religious aspect of the Hussite movement was almost always overlooked: "With sword and spirit, it was a Czech who was first to fight for the freedom of all Europe—not only for his own freedom but for all nations." "The Czech nation was the first in Europe to undertake the grand battle for freedom from absolutism."[4]

At the opposite pole of this contradictory Czech perception, Europe is defined entirely differently—as a different world than the Czech one, a world that is foreign, hostile, even "inhuman," as a world with which a battle must be waged for one's independence. According to the logic of this second statement, national self-confidence does not need support in the European context because the Czech question is of great import and will assert itself perforce not only "outside Europe" but even "against it." Once again, the quotation from the Vítkov

---

* "Dear Gentlemen. Europe is watching."

memorial has its parallel in several utterances of the time. The Czech poet Rudolf Mayer appeals to "the Czech tribe" with the words "you did not tremble before Europe." The journalist Jan Erazim Sojka asserts along the same lines, "All of Europe trembled before of the tremendous might of the Czechs."[5] Such statements are likewise linked to a notion of Czech identity, and within this framework it assumes the form of medieval Hussite chiliasm presented in the form of contemporary national values: the worth of national community ought to be in its striving toward difference, in its daring to defend (even in spite of Europe) "its truth."

For all this, however, the dissimilarity between the two types of expression is not absolute. Of course, the transition from one to the other could, but did not necessarily have to, denote any actual change in cultural orientation. Both the acceptance of Europe as an appropriate context for Czech matters as well as the perception of Europe as a foreign and hostile world served a single goal: to demonstrate the special and important values of the Czech question. In the first case, the argument for national independence is the sharing of common values with Europe. We Czechs are valuable in our distinctiveness because even we recognize the same European cultural axiology or even because in us European values are concentrated in the purest form. In the second case, it is precisely the difference and independence from the European context that is argued for (we Czechs are valuable for our distinctiveness, because we are different from Europe).

At the same time, one finds in these apparently contradictory sentiments—exemplified by the expression noted by Tomek and the memorial on Vítkov Hill—a definite project for a different and better future, a call for self-improvement, which surprisingly also links the two sentiments. Let us be more perfect, more original, more valuable, whether by fulfilling the needs and desires of Europe, as in the shout of the man on a Prague street during the Pentecostal storms, or by being ourselves, independent of Europe, different from it. The space demarcated by these two pronouncements is simply a space of ambiguity. The statement that interprets Europe as its own context for the Czech question, to which events of the "Czech world" are and should be compared, and according to which they should be "read," at the same time regards Europe as something external, apart, something that at most "looks" at them only from the outside. Furthermore, the statement that presents Europe in the role of the opponent, even a defeated enemy in Hussite battles in the distant past, carries within itself implicit or perhaps even explicit admiration of Europe: Europe—plentiful, rich, "ironclad," in contrast to the Czech lands—poor, few in number, footslogging, and yet it noticed us. In practice, it is rather difficult to ascertain whether a certain cultural assertion contains a pro- or an anti-European sentiment. For example, if Karolína Světlá* programmatically creates her Czech national types from the Podještědí region as bearers of European spiritual traumas, should this be seen as a sign of the evident Europeanism of the Czech lands, a Europeanism that has reached its furthest and most remote corners?[6] Or, on the contrary, is it a rejection of Europe and its cultural debates, as in "We do not need Europe, it has nothing to teach us, and that which Europe is now discovering with such avidity has been part of us for a long time"?

The Czech world is simply obsessed with the desire to be seen and appreciated by Europe, even when it is ostensibly ignoring it. The Czech world also readily presents its own values both as independent and at the same time highly valued by Europe. In grandiloquent verse, poets praised Josef Jungmann,[†] the nineteenth-century Czech National Revivalist: "His genius is so great / that half of Europe / admires him." Of the forged manuscripts[‡] they wrote: "Europe celebrates their glory / and rejoices in their eminence," and so on. [7] On the other hand when the "Czech world" declares itself to be "European," it does not try to hide its desire for dissimilarity and otherness.

In both cases, it is a matter of defining Czech identity as possessing special and peculiar values. Thus, it is not surprising that in the strategic emphasis on Czech individuality, we find alongside the European context another one—a common Slavic context to which the Czech world can refer. This of course has great significance for the Czech national emancipation project: The European attribute was not separated from the German cultural environment and could be used only in ritualized arguments of the type "We are not worse, we are not less civilized, independent, cultural—we are not less European than you, Germans." On the contrary, the Slavic attribute meant radical separation: "We are different from Germans, we belong to another, Slavic world, which has a different past and more importantly a different future." The Slavic world is presented as possessing a different value system, yet at the same time as a world that also possesses

---

* Karolína Světlá (1830–99) was a Romantic Czech novelist and feminist.

† Josef Jungmann (1773–1847) was a linguist, poet, and translator. He systematically adapted words from other Slavic languages to Czech. Along with Josef Dobrovský, he is considered to be a creator of the modern Czech language.

‡ Václav Hanka (1791–1861), a Czech writer and linguist, along with his friend Josef Linda (1792–1834) forged the so-called Zelenohorský and Královédvorský manuscripts, claiming they were medieval writings that demonstrated the noble lineage of Czech literature. See the chapter "Mystification and the Nation" in this book for more on this topic.

traditional European values. In fact, it personifies Europe in a more authentic and pure form, whereas modern Europe has abandoned these values.

These two spheres of the emblematics of Europe meet and sometimes even intersect. At one pole (the one that claims Europe), Europe is conventionally characterized—by the attribute of "freedom," which appeared as a component of the theme of Europe as early as 500 BC in ancient Greece during the wars between Greece and "Asian" Persia. After the French Revolution, this theme once again emerges via the attribute of Christianity, which became a fixed component in meditations on Europe during the Middle Ages, as well as an Enlightened attribute of civilization, and so on.[8]

At the other pole (the one that rejects Europe), we see a different process. Sometimes, depending on their goals, Czechs see themselves as quintessentially European, at other times wholly different. From this perspective, two allegorical poems by Svatopluk Čech* are revealing. They portray an image of Europe as "an argosy of spirits," from whose sails "waft the plague" and the red color of blood; the ship's crew is at odds with each other due to their irreconcilable points of view regarding the improvement of Europe, and in the end they bring their ship to ruin.[9] The ship *Slavie*, on the other hand, sails toward a happy future. The traditional European motif of "Christianity" and its values is negated: Europe appears as a community turned away from God (this motif is emphasized by the story of a priest ridiculed and then put to death by a crowd).

The theme of civilization is denied by the image of chaos; the theme of freedom is seen as hunger for blood and violence. The traditional "European attributes" have clearly shifted to and become part of the Slavic value system. This holds for the traditional European attribute of Christianity (it is through the Slavs, "the poverty-stricken of humanity, / that Christ's clear Gospel will resound"), as well as for the attribute of freedom as projected in the mythologized image of the ideal Proto-Slavic community, which serves as model for the future "family ties" of Slavic nations. Finally, it holds for the attribute of civilized behavior. Slavism is presented as a new civilization ("the morning star of new worlds"), different from the civilized and cultivated nature of Europe beneath whose "grinning mask of humanity" is hidden "the bared fangs of vehement malice."

From this perspective, even *Slavie*'s traditionally negative attributes, such as material and cultural "poverty," become positive, even Evangelical values, for

---

* Svatopluk Čech (1846–1908) was the patriotic Czech poet and novelist who espoused Pan-Slavism.

they recall Christ's indigence and humiliation ("so poor you are," "scorned, with radiant, bespitten vestments").[10] Poverty came to mean inner richness and new and higher values that were more precious than those ever provided by Europe. In the poem, Europe is symptomatically identified with the West and *Slavie* with the East.

In this confrontation, Slavs and Slavism are seen as a new youthful value, whereas Western Europe is "aging, languishing"; it is a decrepit civilization without a future, doomed to destruction.[11] The attribute of "newness" in the theme of *Slavie* as a counterpart to Europe was placed on the same level with the theme of America, which in the nineteenth century is often likewise juxtaposed to Europe as "a new continent," historically predestined to overcome dissipated European life forms. Of course, opposed to America (which is identified with the United States and seen as the embodiment of inorganic transformation and the truncation of spiritual values in the name of material progress) a new Slavic civilization is invoked, perceived primarily as a return to its roots, original values, to nature and fundamental human relationships—to poetry.[12] "The entire Slavic nation is a poet," says Sojka, and this characterization directly symbolizes the effort to replace the prestigious values attributed to Europe (technology, rich and thought-provoking literature) with another value, immeasurable and absolute.[13]

These two positions obviously reflect the influence of Russian Slavophilism, which programmatically viewed Europe with distrust. Incidentally, Svatopluk Čech's verses, "Behold, the East in beauteous radiance / It kisses my breast like a warm breeze—/ and Europe expires like a vague dream, / I bid you farewell in the murky distance," seem to paraphrase the verses of the Russian Slavophile Aleksei Khomiakov, "the West, shrouded and plunged in darkness: / You, the East, having known that fate, / arise in a new radiance, / cast away the darkness!"[14] Among the Czechs, Slavism was seen just as it was by the Russian Slavophiles, as a value to replace the European world or at least immensely rejuvenate it. In an indirect polemic against the metaphor by the German historian Leopold von Ranke (who characterized Europe as a "Germanic-Romance marriage" in which Slavism was relegated to the sad role of an intruder) in the Czech context on the contrary, the theme of the marriage of Europe and the Slavs is promoted.[15] In a poem by Josef Wenzig, Europe is apostrophized as a girl who rejected as a husband a Persian who bit "in desperate passion / her fair Greek leg," as well as an Arab who kissed her "Spanish face," but also a Mongol and a Turk. Then she is summoned by "a worthy claimant / brave, handsome, noble / from the east / whom she would marry with reverence."[16]

Of course, a certain patheticization of Slavism and an anticipation of its future historical role appeared in other countries, as well, whether accompanied by fear or simple curiosity. In the development of Czech literature, as previously discussed, even a German observer could hear talk of a "newly emerging world with its prophetic tongues."[17] The patheticization of Slavism was also cultivated as part of the Czechs' own messianism, which was perhaps less thoroughgoing than Russian, Polish, or Slovak messianism, yet it possessed a clear vision of a different European arrangement of affairs and a different future role for the Czech nation. Usually such open manifestations of messianism were restricted to private statements by individuals, but in a certain way this imbued them with more weight by placing them beyond the realm of literary stratagems and casting them into the "genre" of private, candid testimony. For example, the Czech patriot Jan Helcelet writes to his friend Matěj Mikšíček about the nation's future and the new organization of Europe, about the inevitable war that will "herald a new historical era in Eastern Europe": "The individual is like a leaf in a forest. The leaves fall and blossom anew, and the forest continues to grow even though so many leaves lie scattered and strewn about the ground. Thus let us turn green happily, while it is our time; if a storm comes, we will not ask who is being torn from the tree, and God willing it will be seen that the forest did not lie idle when it was turning green."[18]

Thus, after the war and especially after the Communist putsch of February 1948, anti-European speeches are not merely heterogeneous ideological contraband. The image of Europe was transformed into "a casemate,"[19] "a metropolitan crater" at the bottom of which writhes "fossilized men and the wreckage of women . . . before life decays in them," the world "of pyramids of air-raid shelters" (whose age and perishing on the threshold of destruction here is clearly symbolized by the metaphor of ancient Egypt) is of course now confronted with positive attributes of the world of socialism. Against the vision "of their future depopulated world" is placed life under socialism, where "everything is vigorously taking wing"; a new era is juxtaposed to the fading sun of the West, which on the contrary "like the sun is rising / into the sky of the young classes, / the young nations of the world." In euphonious parallel, Western "decaying" is set against Eastern "healing."[20]

Europe is presented here not as a complex unit sharing the same values but as a territory to be conquered ("already the march of the proletariat is thundering throughout Europe").[21] Europe is abandoned for another cultural community, which, despite both geography and historical conditions, should link nations of the world that adhere to the same worldview, whether it is called "the camp of peace," "the camp of socialism," or the Orwellian Eurasia ("The magnificent joyous song / of a hundred million people above the sixth continent / the spring of Eurasia").[22] At the same time, one cannot help but notice that behind this ideology, which ostentatiously declared itself to be original, was merely an updated version of bygone rhetoric. Not only was this rhetoric not without domestic precedent, but it was in fact closely connected with the methods of defining Czech identity in the preceding century. World War II could be easily interpreted as a victorious war of the Slavs over the hostile German element, as a fulfillment of ancient prophecies whose image Helcelet described in his letter.

After the war, various leftist propagandistic initiatives also proceeded along these lines. The entire postwar discussion of the theme of the cultural orientation between "the West" and "the East," whether the individual voices unequivocally supported the East or searched for a much more circumspect formulation of the cultural problem of the Czech lands and of the entirety of Czechoslovakia, evoked the earlier themes of the nineteenth century on the ascendant age of Slavism, the links of Czech culture to Slavic and especially Russian culture, but also the themes of the "dissipation," "corruption," and moral depravity of the West, especially Europe. Admittedly, the confrontation could be circumvented by proclaiming Russia and the Soviet Union as the "inheritors of the West," as the only genuine, authentic Europe: "The true Europe, the Europe of the best and highest traditions, exists today in the Soviet Union, which took as its foundation the greatest and historically most significant achievement of nineteenth-century European culture—the teachings of Marx and Engels."[23] Precisely in this way, however, the opposition between Europe and the East was completed. The East became a solitary island in an ocean of European and, more generally, Western decadence, so that only here (with the requisite shifts in value) was it possible to preserve original Western values and transport them into the world of tomorrow.

Meditations on Central Europe were developed on the basis of previous stratagems regarding the Slavic argument. Even before the beginning of the 1970s, we find this concept in the reflections of a number of Czech journalists, essayists, and historians, and it was backed up by a rich history, especially within German and Austro-German political thought.[24] We find it formulated perhaps most clearly by Friedrich Naumann during World War I,[25] when it was employed to ideologically reflect the reality of the war ("Mitteleuropa ist Kriegsfrucht. Zusammen . . . haben wir gekämpft, zusammen wollen wir leben!"* says Naumann).[26] An awareness of this tradition, however, is practically nonexistent in debates among Czech exiles and dissidents. It was as if the concept of Central

---

* "Central Europe is the fruit of war. Together we fought, together we want to live."

Europe was born anew, as some sort of personal reaction to the trauma of the crushing of the Prague Spring in 1968. To a certain extent, it is presented as a nostalgically tinged theme. Like the concept "Europe," "Central Europe" is more than a neutral geographic term, and it is also more than a geopolitical term, as it was primarily in the case of Naumann's "Mitteleuropa."

For the historian Jan Křen, Central Europe represents a "strange, stormy, tragic, and vital subcontinent."[27] Milan Kundera sees its vitality especially in the Central European "passion for variety"[28] in which the essence of Europeanism is even more evident in this new period ("Europe can sustain diversity," says the politician Petr Pithart).[29] Milan Šimečka also saw the uniqueness of Central Europe in its composite nature "where nations lived," within an amalgam of "influences, languages, and traditions," which "created the values of Europe's previous greatness."[30] He sees it as a space in which "the grand events of history intervene in our lives."[31] Here, the concept of Central Europe is clearly being juxtaposed primarily with the notion of Eastern Europe: "Eastern Europe is shifting sands . . . the fragile edge of the European continent, a crumbling edge falling away and disappearing from Europe. I understand Eastern Europe as a fully realized 'spiritual Balkanization,' Central Europe as a sober, skeptical, but nevertheless tenacious will for synthesis."[32] At the same time, Central Europe is often understood as something almost extinct, as a cultural center whose irretrievable loss has distorted Europe and has in fact thrown it dangerously off balance. By denying its own center, in such argumentation, Europe itself seemed to be losing its meaning. Central Europe is thus understood namely as the most intrinsic personification of the European essence, as the "heart" of Europeanism. The diversity of Central Europe, perceived almost as a genetic property, is offered as a defense against unification, to which Western Europe has already succumbed, as well as against monolithic, muzzled Russia. Potentially, Central Europe is (or rather was) something endlessly polymorphous and alive.

Even authors who attempted to oppose this mythologization of Central Europe (Josef Kroutvor, for example), instead of offering a sober analysis of the concepts and rhetoric connected with it, sought instead a completely different evaluative variant of the same mythologized image: "In Central Europe everything is flat, neatly leveled, subordinated to the general mean. People avoid extremes and display no interest in them. The Biedermeier tradition has outlived all regimes, fashions, and styles. The golden middle route is the route of Central Europe." Central Europe is in this case perceived as a middle space between the historical dynamism of the West and the "inactivity" of Russia, a space in which—to quote Kroutvor—primarily reigns absurdity.[33]

But in both images—Central Europe as the quintessence of Europeanism and its opposite, that of Central Europe as an empire of permanent Biedermeier—the methods of mythologization created in the nineteenth century are once again activated. Concerning Czech and Slovak National Revival culture, reference here is made (positive or negative) to a special signification attributed to the very notion of "center" and a nation's location therein.[34] With the center as the supreme value—a value free from imperfect, peripheral phenomena, from all extremes—patriotic intellectuals argued on behalf of the nations and languages of the Slavs, and later especially on behalf of the Czech nation and language. The presence in the center of whatever spectrum of phenomena—the central position of the pronunciation of a sound, the central position of a language among other languages, the central position of a nation vis-à-vis other nations—automatically becomes a positive ideological value. A position off center became a negative one. Moreover, it was not important what type of "center" was under consideration. In the geographic sense, for example, the Slavs became the nation of the center because their territory occupied a position between the Greeks (the prestigious nation of antiquity) and the Germans (the immediate opponents to the emancipation of the Czech nation) or perhaps another prestigious nation of contemporary Europe. At other times, the Slavs' medium or moderate height was adduced as a positive value because it was understood as a "central position" and thus a quality to which the Czech nation must aspire in its self-development. Furthermore, conscious modifications of the Czech language were initiated, for example, from the perspective of its melodiousness.

Soon the role of "mediation" or "brokerage" becomes superimposed on this layer of rhetoric. The task of the nation of the center, its "historical purpose," becomes the role of cultural mediator, the unifier of various cultural influences (for example, František Palacký's* "mutual interpenetration of Roman, German, and Slavic elements in Europe"). Frequently, this role was associated with the Czechs' central position on the European continent. Their geographic central position is also perceived as the center of values, as the "heart" of the continent. The Czech lands "sparkle like a rose . . . in the heart of Europe," "they lie in the heart of Europe, where almost all the cultures of our continent intersect." They appear as the very "historical heart of Europe."[35]

After August 1968, the Revivalist mythologization of the "center" became a natural breeding ground for Czech rhetoric pertaining to "Central Europe." It is

---

* František Palacký (1798–1876) was a Czech historian and politician. He is considered the founder of modern Czech historiography. His chief work is *The History of the Czech Nation in Bohemia and Moravia* (5 vols., 1836–76).

paradoxical but at the same time typical that Milan Kundera's attempt to come to grips precisely with this Revivalist mythology stands at the beginning of this discussion. In his article "Czech Destiny," Kundera clearly characterizes the traditional Revivalist ideograms in a skeptical manner: "The Czech National Revival which, at the center of feverish Europe, floundered atop its own small sand-hill, a Revival which rapped Mácha's* knuckles with its pedant's ruler, a Revival incapable of forging values relevant to greater humankind, a Revival full of trifling acts and devoid of great deeds."[36] At another level, however, Kundera thunderously accepts the Revivalist rhetoric, as Václav Havel noticed in his response to the article.[37] Kundera develops the traditional Revivalist motif of the "small nation" that achieves greatness—something that comes automatically to large nations—only with strenuous spiritual striving and creation. He writes of the "fateful" union between the Czech nation and culture, and finally he sees even August 1968 from that perspective. The ideogram of the "center" appears here, too, as a part of his conceptual register: we stood in "the center of world history."

Not even in his response to Havel's critique did Kundera abandon the sphere of Revivalist discourse. On the contrary, he lodged himself even more firmly and unequivocally within it. Again he stressed the ancient theme of the "Czech center": "The Czech nation has always been the crossroads of European traditions." Furthermore, he refused to see in this motif a mere Revivalist illusion; on the contrary, it was the key to understanding one's own "geographic and historical possibilities."[38]

It is only against the background of discussions of the theme of the National Revival—which at the same time brought to the fore Revivalist ideograms—that Kundera's theme of "Central Europe" later emerges. The editors of *Svědectví* were obviously aware of this because they began their overview of the debate precisely with the issue of the National Revival—by using the previously mentioned essay by Kundera, Havel's subsequent reply, and Kundera's response to Havel. Here, Kundera offers the theme of Central Europe simply as a theoretical development of this hypothetical Czech and Czechoslovak geographic and historic (central) possibility without perhaps realizing that he was not departing from the language of the Revivalist myth. For Kundera and the other participants in the debate, the theme of "Central Europe" as a peculiar cultural phenomenon remained primarily in that magical realm of the emblem of the "center," which at

---

* Karel Hynek Mácha (1810–36) was the first (and only) Czech Romantic poet. *May* (1836) is his greatest work.

the beginning of the Czech National Revival accompanied positive "Czech" values as an argument for the Czechs' exclusivity. Forgotten, lost in the Austrian monarchy, the Czech lands rose in significance, albeit only at the level of semiotic activity. The central position could be glorified, worshipped, and celebrated without regard to the problematic present. Thereby, a nation previously scorned could be presented as a nation and its territory that lay at the very epicenter of events. Here are the Czech sources of the notion of Central Europe, revived by Kundera's essays as well as by those of other Czech exile and "samizdat" publicists and historians of the 1970s and '80s. Central Europe became an independent value precisely because of its union with the Revivalist appraisal of the central position, with Revivalist mythology and also the rhetoric of the "center." Remarks concerning the cultural region characterized by the wish for "synthesis," the Central European passion "for variety," the Central European "entwining of influences, languages, and traditions" only appear to contradict the Revivalist attempt to create a coherent and uninterrupted Czech tradition using foreign remnants. In reality, and at a different level, they repeat the Revivalist remarks, which placed all things Czech (Slovak, Slavic) above any sort of bias. Remarks concerning the "sobriety" of this region also have their roots here—whether in Pithart's positive sense or in Kroutvor's ironic denial of the Central European legend. After all, even Kroutvor's scathing formulations refer directly to (even if with grotesque, parodic exaggeration) an important component of the Revivalist rhetoric of the center, the center as an average or norm, as excluding extremes.

In other words, erstwhile rhetorical means are projected onto current or contemporary deliberations concerning the value and meaning of a cultural region, a means whose point was never to reflect the whole, to reflect the productive collaboration of nations and cultures, but rather to construct an illusion relevant to a single nation.

Similar to the themes of "Europeanism" and "Slavism," the theme of "Central Europeanism" is likewise primarily an attribute of Czech self-demarcation and even self-assessment with regard to other nations. Whereas "Europeanism" was an emblem proclaiming the Czech nation on equal footing with other European nations (especially the Germans, because this is what it was really about), Slavism proclaimed a Czech "differentiation" from the Germans. "Central-Europeanism" carries with it the motif of a special meaning of the Czech cultural space (as a central space, a space suitable for synthesis, a space preserving the essence, which has already died out on the disintegrating edges). In the confrontation with Russia (and when the discussion of Central Europe came up in the 1970s and

'80s, it was all about differentiation from "Russia"), this attribute was more-over sufficiently differential. With regard to Germany, this differential element was losing its function. The theme of Central Europe sounded originally like an ideal vision of the interpenetration of ethnically diverse cultures and their cross-fertilization. If at least this aspect of the Revivalist need for self-demarcation and self-assessment was suppressed, in practice we see on the contrary attempts to unite the image of Central Europe with the Czech lands more closely. We even find such attempts in the words of the traditional demythologizer Havel, whose current political position sometimes forces him to resort to established stereo-types: "We live at the very centre of Central Europe."[39] At the same time, we follow with jealous and ironic attention the attempts of other nations to usurp the claim to the center of Europe. We do not want to admit that interest in the "center" is generally widespread and not exclusively our cultural possession. The Germans claimed this right long ago. At least from the time of Friedrich Ludwig Jahn (1778–1852), they considered themselves the *Mittelwolk*, "the old and honorable nation of the center in Europe," and they insist on this self-characterization to this day.[40]

Recently, such attempts have been revived in Slovakia. In a contest by the League for the Advancement of the Slovak Nations, names such as In the Heart of Europe, Land in the Heart of Europe, The Heart of Europe, and The Center of Europe repeatedly appeared as suggestions for a symbolic Slovak designa-tion.[41] The motif of the center appeared on T-shirts (Slovakia—The Heart of Europe) and was also conspicuously revived in Slovak independence ceremo-nies. Consider the lighting of fires in a village declared as the actual geographic center of Europe (incidentally, on Czech tourist maps the geographic center is situated near the border with Germany in the area of Mariánské Lázně, whereas Lithuanians contend the center of Europe lies 25 kilometers from Vilnius in east-ern Lithuania not far from the village of Bernotai).[42] In passing, we should note that even non-European nations manipulate the notion of the center while char-acterizing their own identity ("We Israelites have the privilege of living at the crossroads of Eastern and Western cultures and can draw from both").[43] And European nations that, because of their geographic location, are excluded from aspiring to the center of the continent frequently construct their identity around another geographic idea of the center.[44]

Of the three geographic attributes of Czech identity, the "Slavic" attribute, so important in the nineteenth century, has recently lost its appeal and is per-ceived as completely discredited by past ideological manipulations—by recent Communist and even older Revivalist maneuvers. Nevertheless, its substitution by Celtic identity, so popular in recent years, has been undertaken in the spirit of Revivalist mythopoeia and therefore cannot escape it. Just as the ritual battles for the center and the parading of one's own "Central Europeanism" did not depart from the fundamentals of Revivalist rhetoric, neither does the (semiotic) play with the "European" argument in any fundamental way depart from the substratum of bygone illusions of the myth of the nation—certainly not when they are linked to the semiotic self-promotion of other nations, such as the Russians, Slovaks, South Slavic nations, Bulgarians, and others: We are Europe—they are Asia, the Balkans, and so on.

4

The Center

The concept of the "center" played a central role in the development of Czech Revivalist thought throughout the eighteenth and nineteenth centuries. This applied not only to the geographic location of the Czechs at the "center of Europe," but also to the middle location of the Slavs between the Germans and the Greeks, and even to the central location of the Czech language between logic and aesthetics.

During the process of Czech cultural creation, there emerged the question of Czech philosophy. In the beginning, the question did not appear to go beyond a purely linguistic need to create specialized terminology and style. "Czech philosophy" appeared as a problem only in the 1840s, when translation methods were no longer taken for granted and when questions arose concerning the originality or the practical contributions of Czech philosophical works, and when even the very usefulness of philosophy as a science for Czech culture was cast into doubt. Despite this highlighting of the problem—ideologically motivated by the conflict with German culture—it did not mean that during Josef Jungmann's* time philosophy was not profoundly useful to the culture of the Czech National Revival. It is not our intention here to discuss the development of Czech philosophical thought but rather to examine the essence of the Czech Revivalist cultural type. Therefore, what will be of interest is a type of philosophy that was not considered philosophy per se, that is, a type not yet present in Czech Revivalist literature as an independent discipline, but instead distributed throughout Josef Jungmann's syncretic cultural activity.

In this activity, the philosophy of Johann Gottfried von Herder[†] played an important role, just as it did in other Slavic nations. Revivalists examined the

---

* Josef Jungmann (1773–1847) was a linguist, poet, and translator. He systematically adapted words from other Slavic languages to Czech. Along with Josef Dobrovský, he is considered to be a creator of the modern Czech language.
† Johann Gottfried von Herder (1744–1803) was a German philosopher who developed the notion of the *volk-nation*, according to which every nation was an organic whole. His thought played a large role in the development of Romanticism throughout Europe.

connections of Herder's conception of humanity with the domestic Slavic "humanitarian" tradition. Thus far, however, what has escaped the attention of Slavic and Bohemist scholars are the very interesting relationships between Herder's philosophical concept of "the center" and the term "center" as employed in scientific, journalistic, and artistic texts at the height of the Czech National Revival.

The term "center" is an important element in Herder's philosophy: "a golden mean," a positive value that excludes extremes and combines within itself all the positive qualities appropriate to a given sphere. It appears at the most diverse levels of Herder's system. Earth is for Herder "a star among stars," tied to the sun, "to its center," and at the same time "it is one of the central planets . . . with regard to its location, size, proportionality, and the duration of its revolution around its own axis and around the sun; every extreme—the largest and smallest, fastest and slowest—is distanced from it on both sides."[1] This central position of Earth likely influenced forms of life here, both plants and animals, among which, again, man is "a creature of the center," in whom are concentrated "a majority of the most delicate rays made from forms similar to him" and in whom is combined "everything that could be combined."[2] But even within the framework of humanity, the category of the center serves as an evaluative element differentiating nations of "beautiful body" residing in "the central region, which lies among two extremes as beauty itself."[3] The center is always connected with variety, with the unification of varieties, and with variation within unity.

Josef Jungmann found Herder's conception of "the center" satisfactory in many respects if only because it corresponded to his tendency toward mysticism, an undifferentiated unified vision of the world, and consequently even toward thinking in analogies. Herder's concept of "the center" was clearly connected to ancient mythological systems and thus could become a compositional element of Josef Jungmann's ideology.[4] In its least symptomatic form, the concept of the center appears in works that attempt to capture the place of humans in relation to nature and to the world in the widest sense. Thus, for example, Antonín Jungmann* characterized a person "as the crucial link or the center of animals," as a being that "among the various largeness and smallness of animals, occupies the average, being more than five feet tall."[5] Jan Svatopluk Presl characterized a person as the "middle and image of all creatures, the most harmoniously

---

* Antonín Jan Jungmann (1775–1854) was the younger brother of Josef Jungmann. A doctor and translator of Czech from German, he assisted his brother in creating new Czech specialized terminology.

proportioned," and František Palacký* called the entire human race "the intermediary between god and worms."[6]

The most interesting and original usage of Herder's philosophical concept, however, lies elsewhere. It is where the concept of the center is no longer accepted from the outside, but where it is most closely tied to the very essence of Revivalist thought, which, precisely for its notion of the "central position" and its values, resorts to Herder's formulation only secondarily. Herder's "center" in this case is no longer an influencing factor and becomes rather a mere instrument of Josef Jungmann's cultural activity.

In this form, the notion of the center was frequently used to evaluate European nations and languages, and nationalist circles employed this concept to argue in favor of Slavic nations and languages. The location in the center, the central location of language, the central location of the nation, and so on automatically became a positive evaluative quality. A position outside the center was associated with a lower or outright negative evaluation. At the same time, what was meant objectively by the center was not important. It could mean the center of a geographic space (the Slavic nation "related to German and Greek and always residing between them"[7]) or the central articulation position in the oral cavity[8] or the understanding of Slavs as being of "average" or "moderate" height. To be sure, in some cases—within the framework of the program to refine the Slavic language—the central position was not accepted as already attained, but rather as a value to which the Slavic language (and therefore the nation) was only now aspiring. Nevertheless, it was a value that was achievable precisely by the Slavs. Ján Kollár,† for example, placed the ideal of perfecting the language at the very center, between logic and aesthetics. To this end, he argued for altering the Czech language to make it more melodious.[9]

On this fundamental level of the mystic center are placed still other values in the texts of the Josef Jungmann period and later.[10] In particular, the role of mediation or agency is emphasized, which results from the application of the concept of the center in its geographical sense. The role of cultural intermediary fulfilled the task of the "nation of the center." This thesis appears in the ideology of the

---

* František Palacký (1798–1876) was a Czech historian and politician. He is considered the founder of modern Czech historiography. His chief work is *The History of the Czech Nation in Bohemia and Moravia* (5 vols., 1836–76).

† Ján Kollár (1793–1852) was a Slovak poet, prose writer, and Pan-Slavist. His most famous work, *Sláva dcery* (Daughter of Sláva, 1824), a cycle of Petrarchan sonnets glorifying the history of the Slavs and lamenting their present state, made him famous throughout the Slavic world.

Czech National Revival early on. We find it as early as the programmatic declaration of the journal *Krok*: "Our placement among other nations, the episodes of
our people and the culture we have hitherto acquired, prove to us that our calling is to transfer European culture to other cultured Slavic nations."[11] František
Palacký developed this thesis in his concept of the significance of Czech history
in *The History of the Czech Nation in Bohemia and Moravia* (1836–67). According to Palacký, the location of Bohemia at the "center and heart of Europe" made
the Czech nation "a center in which the various elements and principles of the
Neo-European national, state, even church life were combined and united, but
not without a battle. In particular one can behold clear and longstanding conflict,
but also an interweaving of Roman, German, and Slavic elements in Europe."[12]
According to this concept, the Czech nation was given a historical role "to serve
as a bridge between the Germans and Slavs, between East and West, and amidst
Europe in general."[13]

At the peak of the Czech National Revival, this ideological system was promoted with a forced matter-of-factness in many journalistic and artistic texts:
"Our Czech lands, round, bordered by mountains—like a lovely rose in the heart
of Europe it reposes"; "In the heart of Europe it sparkles like a rose"; "Bohemia,
that graceful rosebud lying in the heart of Europe, is especially suited to be
the center of literary exchange, and, yes, perhaps the core of the large trunk of
culture, branching throughout the entirety of Europe. Here is the first meridian
dividing the great firmament of literature into two hemispheres."[14] The union
between the idea of the center with the concept of the Czech nation, however,
was in no way direct or provided by the geographic position of the Czech lands
alone. On the one hand, it emerged from the myth of the center as a positive
and Slavic value. The concept of the center was preserved in its purest form in
Kollár's *Slávy Dcera*: "In the center of the universe," in the center of millions
of "planetary systems" was located Kollár's Slavic sky.[15] At the same time, this
was a polemic with analogous national applications of Herder in the German
milieu, for example Theodor Rohmer or F. L. Jahn, who characterized the German nation as "das alte ehrwurdige Mittelvolk Europas."*[16] Even here one can
see a manifestation of the "translatorial" construction of Czech culture in relation to German.

When using the term center in its geographic sense, it tended to be seen as a
definite synthesis, as a concentration of qualities that were not of the center.
According to Palacký, the values of the Roman and German world permeated

---

* German for "the old venerable *Mittelvolk* of Europe."

and joined the Slavic ones in the "central" historical location of the Czech nation. Situating the Slavs in the center, between the Greeks and the Germans, was linked to the idea of the blending of the best national and linguistic qualities of the Hellenic and German worlds (for example, the connection of aesthetics with logic).[17] This conception of the center as a concentration of the best qualities, which found support and formulation in Herder, was connected in the thought of Josef Jungmann's generation to the generally accepted cult of synthesis. In Jungmann's system, Slavic was always characterized as a single whole that unified a number of qualities and values present outside of the Slavic region only individually and thus in truncated form. It is no coincidence that at that time, Mattias Bel's* statement was again made topical in the introduction to Pavel Doležal's *Grammatica Slavico-Bohemica* (Slavic-Bohemian Grammar) (1746). The characteristic qualities of Spanish (seriousness, magnificence), French (grace, fluency), English (dignity, effectiveness), German (semantic richness, firmness), Italian (softness, melodiousness), and Hungarian (authoritative severity) were assigned also to Czech. Thus, synthesis was sought in the Slavic world as a whole. To guarantee its inner differentiation and diversity, it was then possible to consider the division into various nations and "dialects." Within the framework of this conception, the individual Slavic nations or languages were given the task of representing and replacing several primary European languages. Thus arose more or less fixed relationships between certain Slavic and non-Slavic languages (nations). The German nation was usually "represented" in the Slavic world by the Czechs, the Italians by the southern Slavs, the French by the Poles, and so on.[18] This conception—even though it could have denied the right to independent national existence of those Slavic nations for whom an adequate analogy was not found in the non-Slavic world (for example for the Slovaks, Ukrainians, and so on)—necessarily counted on the positive evaluation of the "multidialecticality" and linguistic fragmentation of the Slavs, which significantly intersected with the political aspirations of Josef Jungmann's generation. At the same time, the ideal of synthesis penetrated into the areas of literature and literary criticism as well. In the Czech milieu, this facilitated the peaceful coexistence of entirely opposing poetic tendencies within a single concept of literature. According to Jungmann's generation, the guarantee of a developed literature was the absorption of various impulses.[19] Kollár formulated this conception eloquently: "The Slavic, especially Czech, language is so fortunate that it may freely move

---

* Mattias Bel (1684–1749) was a Slovak historian, philosopher, pedagogue, and scientist. He wrote the introduction to Pavel Doležal's book.

among all poetic forms, old and new, Classical and Romantic: hexameters and alexandrines, pentameters and ottava rima, Saphic verse and sonnets, rhythm, meter, and rhyme."[20]

At the same time, however, the concept of the center was acquiring still other, seemingly antithetical attributes even though they were related to the notion of the center as a synthesis. The center could even appear as a quality whose positive value stemmed not from an accumulation but a rejection of the qualities of liminal phenomena. And as long as this notion was not verbalized with the help of the terms "center, middle," and others, it represented in general form an important component of Revivalist ideology at its peak: the requirement that it reject all extremes appeared in the most varied texts of the time, often in the form of the popular formulation "the golden path of the center": "The golden middle road is the safest and has no need to veer to the edges and remotest parts."[21] Significantly, this notion participated in general to the emergence of an ideal of literature that was above one-sidedness ("a one-sided poem in our literature is something heretofore unheard of"[22]). It also assumed a definitely negative position toward European Romanticism. Perhaps in its most visible form, this notion came to the fore in the field of nascent Czech politics, where it served to justify the empty phrase about the "golden middle road" as a political program.

Herder's center was exploited—and actually manipulated—according to the needs of emerging Czech political thought. In the 1840s, however, especially among the young generation, a different image of reality was gradually brought forward. Although the young generation accepted several aspects of the ideological system of Jungmann's generation, this adoption meant simultaneously the destruction of the supporting pillars of the earlier ideological system. Dynamic components began to penetrate the static conception of the center more and more frequently. If the older notion of the center found appropriate support in Herder, now, when it was becoming dynamic and being introduced to the notion of societal development, it could take full advantage of the stimulus of Hegel's philosophical system, particularly in Augustin Smetana's* own interpretation, informed as it was by the spirit of Czech nationalism, though the author himself did not belong to the nationalist circle: "Of all Slavic nations, ours intrudes furthest into the German territory, and for this reason alone it is indisputably intended to take over German culture (which preceded Slavic culture in the same way as classical preceded German and Oriental preceded the culture of the classical age) and transmit it to the eastern tribes of the Slavs."[23]

---

* Augustin Smetana (1814–51) was a Czech Hegelian philosopher and excommunicated priest.

Already in this statement one can see that the application of the Hegelian triad did not have to disrupt the fundamental semantic layer of the notion of the "center." It was sufficient to reevaluate it with respect to the movement of history. What could remain intact was the notion of the center as mediation and intermediary. But in addition to its older form as an objective and thus ahistorical exchange of cultural assets, a new concept found its way in. Mediation here was understood not as a spatial function, but rather a temporal one, as the transferring of one's cultural inheritance from the past into the future. Similarly, even the notion of the center as a concentration of the best nonmedial qualities was transformed from a static to a dynamic synthesis close to Hegel's conception.

This is evident in the argumentation of the Ľudovít Štúr* generation in Slovakia, even when they were explicitly distancing themselves from Hegel's conception. It is the Štúr generation that most clearly foregrounds the argument that the transition from Herder to Hegel is in no way inorganic and that it is connected with the actual development of philosophical thought. That is, we can assume a direct connection between Herder's concept of the center and Hegel's synthesis.

M. J. Hurban† laid out his philosophy of history in an article titled "Science and Slovak Views." Here, Josef Jungmann's center was completely reassessed. The future Slavic science, which is the subject of the article, is at a higher stage of development than German science, which strives to understand "things and systems." Slavic science is to be the comprehension of "truth in its entirety." The main feature of this future Slavic science was to be the synthetic perception of reality, not as a collection of phenomena, but as a collection of syntheses, such as "intention–deed, glorious–act, glorious–life, defensive–battle, aggressive–peace, glorious–man, world–spirit, world–life–spirit."[24] This concept was further developed by P. K. Hostinský. He proceeds from the conviction that against the one-sided German philosophy (metaphysical) and the similarly one-sided Western European philosophy (physical), the Slavic philosophical project must bridge the fundamental contradictions of reality (matter, carnality–spirit, mind) and open up through their synthesis in the concept of "vision" as a direct cognition of the entire essence, a higher developmental stage of the cognitive process.[25]

Hostinský's interpretation of Hurban clearly shows to what extent the notion of the dynamic, historical synthesis grew from the traditional, spatially demarcated concept of the center. "Vision" appeared to Hostinský as "the illuminated

---

* Ľudovít Štúr (1815–56) was a Slovak politician, journalist, and linguist. He was the most notable advocate of Slovak nationalism during the nineteenth century.
† Miloslav Jozef Hurban (1817–88) was a Slovak writer, Evangelical priest, and politician.

peak of Kriváň* from which the summits of previous philosophies lie deep in the valleys and from which the interior of the future church of Slavic science can be seen."[26] Although the traditional interpretation of the Tatra Mountains as a center is used here,[27] the previous spatial characteristics have vanished in favor of temporal ones.

Perhaps it is not necessary to emphasize this turning of attention to time, to the rhythm of history's motion, which in itself meant a considerable step forward in the Czech and Slovak context. If some members of the younger generation of the 1840s posed the question of the "usefulness" of philosophy for the needs of nascent Czech society, they did not notice one essential thing (and neither did their adversaries), namely, that philosophy (even though it had not become established as "Czech philosophy") had surrounded them for quite some time. Dissolved as it was in Revivalist "Pan-culture," it had fulfilled the most relevant functions in Czech society. It had offered its own language for the expression of their needs and dreams.

* Kriváň, 2,495 meters above sea level, is the fifth-highest mountain in Slovakia.

5

Prague

During the National Revival, the city of Prague for the Czechs and the Tatra Mountains for the Slovaks, respectively, became national symbols. It was around these two symbols that both nations developed their own way of looking at themselves and the world.

During the 1830s and '40s, an image of Prague was born in Czech literature, especially in journalism and prose. It was an image of Prague as a city, and in this sense it was analogous to the images of city life in other established literatures. It was roughly in this manner that Charles Dickens's London and Eugène Sue's Paris arose. Texts of the time reflected the social organism of the city more fully and tangibly than before. At the same time was born an awareness of the aesthetics of the city, which no longer stood in contrast to the countryside but rather appeared as one of its components. At the end of the eighteenth and beginning of the nineteenth century, by comparison, the city was perceived as nonaesthetic and in principle was either passed over in literature or appeared only in negative terms, as a point of departure for an escape into the authenticity of nature ("In the city a person leads an improper life"; "Indeed, I have become weary of / cities, the beautiful houses"[1]). In the 1830s and '40s, the city's picturesque charm was not only discovered but also codified: "From the gray shadows, cities peep out like white flecks and above them circle wisps of smoke."[2]

Even so, the image of Prague formed at this time was not unequivocally the first to appear. Admittedly, this image did not emerge in the same continuous fashion as it did in Western cultures, but it certainly did not arise from naught. At the beginning of the nineteenth century, we see in journalism and especially in village stage comedies a few traces of interest in the life of the city. These traces, however, exemplify the difficulties of promoting interest in the cultural conditions of the National Revival. Village comedies, and in fact theater itself, were located at the margins of Josef Jungmann's* culture and frequently beyond

---

* Josef Jungmann (1773–1847) was a linguist, poet, and translator. He systematically adapted words from other Slavic languages to Czech. Along with Josef Dobrovský, he is considered to be a creator of the modern Czech language.

its purview. The theater, as we shall see, stipulated entirely different parameters due to the necessity of a genuine national/popular public. If in this way moments of genuine city life, especially Prague life, penetrated the culture of the National Revival, they did so via the back door, through the rejected, or at least the less respected, periphery. Even these moments were forced through for the most part from the outside, primarily through the Viennese farce. Even in the most distinctive Czech play with Prague motifs in the 1820s, J. N. Štěpánek's *Alina or Prague in Another Part of the World*, a freely adapted and localized translation of Adolf Bäuerle's *Aline oder Wien in einem anderen Weltteile,** Prague life and institutions had only a slightly more independent character.[3]

Prague life appears here primarily as a mere equivalent of Viennese life, and parts of the play are frequently simply transposed, sometimes almost word for word, except for localizing details. Prague life and institutions were actually created via translation, by *Bohemizing* the original Viennese life and institutions, whether merely on the level of place designations (Prater—Hvězda, Bubeneč, Kohlmarkt—Uhelný trh, Wasserkunstbastei—Vodičkova ulice, Dunaj—Moldava, that is, Vltava, and so on) or on higher thematic levels ("Man sieht eine freie Gegend. Es stellt die Donau vor, links der Kahlen und Leopoldsberg. Im Hintergrunde die weite Aussicht auf den, 'üppigen Strom'";[†] "one sees a Prague bridge across the Moldau, the entire Lesser Town with the Castle and the church"[4]). Even songs were frequently closely affiliated to the original songs' thematics:

Když ty krásné české háje,
když vlast ještě spatřím svou;
rozkošné ty české ráje
protýkané Moldavou.
Všude z hájů, lučin, strání
rozléhá se prozpěvání
Taj ty dla! tu ty dli.
. . . .
Ach v Praze je krásně, ach,
    Praha je má!
Prahu, ach! celý svět Prahu nemá![5]

---

* Adolf Bäuerle (1789–1859) was an Austrian writer. *Alina* was first performed in 1822.
† "One sees an open countryside. There is the Danube, to the left of the Kahlenberg and Leopoldsberg Mountains. The broad view of that 'immense river' fills the background."

[When those beautiful Czech groves,
When my homeland I still behold;
Charming are these Czech paradises
interwoven by the Moldau.
Everywhere from groves, meadows, hillsides
resounds the singing
Tai ti dla! Tu ti dli.
. . . .
Oh it is beautiful in Prague, oh,
    Prague is mine!
Prague, oh! The whole world does not have Prague!]

Noch einmal dies schöne Gegend
meiner heimat möcht' ich sehn,
noch einmal, am heitern Ufer
unsrer Donau möcht' ich stehn!
Kommt ein Schiff mit frischen Leuten,
hört man s'jubeln schon vom weiten:
Jaheiha, ja ih he!
Östreich Vivat und Juhe!
. . . .
Das muss ja prächtig sein,
dort möcht ich bin!
Ja, nur ein Kaiserstadt,
    Ja, nur ein Wien!⁶

[I'd like to see the beautiful region
of my homeland once again,
once again I can stand on the serene
bank of our Danube!
A ship is coming with joyful people,
one can already hear them from far away
shouting with joy:
Yahei ha, yai h he!
Love live Austria, Hooray!
. . . .
It must indeed be splendid,
I would like to be there

Yes, only one imperial city,
Yes, only one Vienna!]

Even though Prague life and institutions were presented in *Alina* primarily from the outside, they were nevertheless presented. They could even develop sporadically within the given framework according to their own logic beyond the space marked out by the original. It was in this area that a substratum emerged, albeit a poor one, on which the Revivalists of the 1830s and '40s could build. Finally, it is symptomatic in this respect that Josef Kajetán Tyl's* farces (especially *Fidlovačka*) referred immediately to *Alina*.

In principle, however, the image of the real Prague and how it developed, especially in the 1830s and '40s, was not obvious or even "correct" for the cultural type of the National Revival at its climax. In its classical form, Revivalist culture did not recognize Prague at all in this image. Jungmann's image was different; it was subordinated to the needs of Revivalist ideology and not at all to the pressure of actual reality, that is, to an aggressive, viable, and quickly developing urban reality.

On the one hand, the image contained a considerable layer of contemporary life and institutions, reflections of the city's everyday life, centers of social life (Kanálka, Krenovy sady, Barvířský ostrov, Nové sady), the social periphery (Uhelný trh, František), and everyday scenes from the lives of inhabitants (the proletariat, street merchants, prostitutes). On the other hand, it contained a different layer altogether, distinguished both by its construction and its collection of motifs. Whereas the "real" layer strives to grasp Prague as a whole in a single unbroken strip, as a sort of conglomeration of concrete details and facts, the other layer—in which classical Revivalist thinking persists—is, from the point of view of geography and sociography, demonstratively discontinuous. It in fact functions with several emblems, stable evaluative signs, which are often arranged in a manifestly ornamental fashion. If among the individual elements of the "real" layer of the image of Prague the relations of classification and combination predominated, the second layer, which was entirely subordinated to the classical evaluative system as characterized by the cultural project of Jungmann's generation, is organized with distinct emphasis on analogy, on the basis of similarities. Its structure is strikingly paradigmatic even though it is syntacticized and laid out on a linear level.

---

* Josef Kajetán Tyl (1808–56) was a dramatist and songwriter. In his play *Fidlovačka*, "Kde domov můj" (Where Is My Home) was heard for the first time and later became the Czechoslovak national anthem. See the first chapter in this book, "Where Is My Home."

Jungmann's register of Prague emblems itself was fairly poor. The concrete Prague locations that entered into it were primarily Vyšehrad and the Vltava River, then Charles Bridge and White Mountain. But even these were described only fragmentarily, even somewhat ostentatiously, without a trace of any sort of local color—not as "images" but rather as "signs." Their characteristics were limited to several elemental sets of thematic attributes that were often not even modified lexically, which, to be sure, sometimes reflected a definite, real, feature (Vyšehrad—"cliff"). At other times they referred to something other than reality (Vltava—"turbid," "staid," "silver-flowing," "aureate").

Also, the sphere of other Prague attributes in the classical Revivalist system is by no means especially large. Prague is partially personified as a female being ("mother," "maiden," "bride," "queen," "widow" of a king). The indivisibleness itself of the image of Prague into a multitude of picturesque and independent motifs in the first quarter of the nineteenth century accommodated similar individualization. This personification, even though it emerged from, on the whole, normal allegorizing methods, is not completely semantically empty. It is symptomatic that the fundamental attributes bring the allegory of Prague closer to the allegory of the nation. The allegory of the nation is similarly connected to the Revivalist symbolism of family ties ("mother," "father," "children"), which clearly shows—in apparent contradiction to the lack of detailed imagery—the significance of Prague in the Revivalist axiology. The urban character of Prague itself was not pertinent to the presence of the city ("the city of Libuše," "the thousand-year seat of the prophetess"). It was reduced to the invariable emblem of "spires" and "the castle." For example, the phrase "hundred-spired Prague" had become fixed as early as the 1920s. The emblem of "fortifications," especially the attribute of "the castle," established a new series of emblems: "the throne" and "the grave" (the royal grave), which were directly connected with a number of others: "altar," "cathedral," and "Mecca of the Czechs."

It is precisely there that interconnectedness occurs, even within the frame of this emblematic layer, on the basis of contiguity, context, and spatial continuation. Here one can clearly see the difference between the two layers, which at that time were based on reflections of Prague. One of them has become the foundation for the interconnectedness of individual Revivalist Prague emblems— the allegorical female figure. Other individual emblems were projected on it: Vyšehrad, but also more generally "the castle," "the towers," "the ramparts" in the shape of a "crown," "diadem," as a decoration of a woman's ("the queen's") head, "the Vltava," along with "Charles Bridge" as an expensive silver belt and "buckle,"[7] "the throne," and so on. Connection was thus built on the basis of similarity; the analogy to a female figure here determined the assemblage of individual motifs and thus replaced their syntactical discontinuousness. The similarity that at first seems to connect the emblems "mother," "woman," "queen," and "(royal) widows" as elements of a single paradigm, of "castle," "spires," "ramparts," "throne," "diadem," "cathedral," "grave," and "Mecca" as elements of another paradigm (possibly of several paradigms closely intertwined) is advocated as a determining force, even in the processes aspiring to a continuous concatenation.

If we depart for a moment from the limitation imposed by a linguistic or general semiotic apparatus, we can sum up the situation by saying that while the "real" layer of Prague's image is directed toward the unending portrayal of the most varied aspects of Prague reality, it is programmatically and demonstratively open. The second layer, Jungmann's layer, of Prague's image is, on the contrary, rigorously closed. It develops inward by the alternation of several analogical attributes, by their movement, which activates a few (but not many) semiotic fields. While the first layer is externally unfixed and nonnormative, in Jungmann's layer only a limited number of canonical motifs are petrified, and only their composition provides a definite measure of freedom.

Therefore, it is not especially surprising that at that time the only local Prague emblem, which was developed into a whole chain of motifs, namely Vyšehrad, in principle did not introduce new attributes into Prague iconography, but represented from only a specific sector with motifs merely hierarchically arranged in a different way. If in the entire iconography of Prague the female element dominates, which naturally does not exclude the incorporation of male attributes of bravery, strength ("sword"), and "power" ("mace," "throne," "castle"), then in the iconography of Vyšehrad, the male element is brought to the forefront, especially in its spheres of "government" (court) and "battle." It is therefore indicative that no matter how unambiguously Prague is classified as belonging to the mythical figure of Libuše, at the same time a very strong reference (at least as a subtext) to Krok and Přemysl* appears in the region of Vyšehrad. Finally, the emphasis on the male element is seen even in the choice of a concrete Vyšehrad motif: the eternal "cliffs," which defy floods of water. In places, the obvious male stylization subordinates even those traditional legendary motifs, which would have appeared at first sight as immune—even the renowned Vyšehrad pillar was

---

* According to legend, chieftain Krok built a castle in what is now Vyšehrad (High Castle) because his wise daughter Libuše prophesied that a great city would emerge there. She married a ploughman named Přemysl and initiated the Přemysl dynasty. She founded Prague in the eighth century.

in its period stylization "a pillar taken from Rome," that is, snatched away from Rome by force.[8] At the same time, Vyšehrad was not allegorized, which alone signifies its lack of independence with respect to Prague. The rest of its emblems, however, are in principle identical: "throne" ("golden seat"), "crown," "castle" (the seat of kings), "ramparts" (walls), and "grave" (funeral urn). The motif of Bílá hora represents a very narrow sector of the entire iconography of Prague, and it is associated primarily with the emblem of the "grave."

Yet another characteristic differentiates the two layers of the image of Prague as it was formed in the 1830s and '40s, namely, the time orientation. Whereas the first is directed at the present, Jungmann's layer accepts the present only as a reflection of the past; in other words, it perceives the present only to the extent to which it is a reflection of the past. All emblems of the classical Revivalist iconography of Prague are directly or indirectly marked by this orientation. From this point of view, the choice of adjectives alone is symptomatic. The emblems "antique" ("old"), "renowned" ("legendary," "famous"), "brave," and "royal" refer directly to the past. Other emblems, which appear neutral from this perspective ("beautiful," "Slavic," "hundred-spired," etc.), refer to it vicariously. Furthermore, other motifs carry a more or less distinctive sign of the past, which is sometimes not expressed but always expressible: "towers" (built in the past), "castle" (built in the past, the former royal castle), "throne" (the former royal throne), "sword" (once made famous in battles), "queen" (surviving the king), the "royal widow," "crown" (the onetime royal crown), and so on.

In its classical Revivalist form, Prague is conceived as "past glory." Whether it is represented by the names of famous historical and mythological figures (Čech, Záboj, Krok, Sámo, Lumír, Žižka, Tycho de Brahe, and others), materialized by its external appearance (historical buildings), or finally merely marked by its external appearance, present-day Prague is seen as a conventional, entirely arbitrary sign of the past that is based solely on the conventions of period usage (even if, perhaps, they have not been historically recorded, or if they are historically questionable or impossible). This orientation of the Revivalist conception of Prague emphasizes, especially in Prague iconography, the emblem of the "grave." Its every emblem was in itself a metaphor of the "grave," the grave of past glory. From the beginning, the perception of present-day Prague as a mere sign of past and lost values carried with it—in accordance with the Pan-European sentimental-Romantic wave, but with a decidedly specific National Revival sense—a nostalgic undertone.[9] This could have been undoubtedly neutralized according to the needs of the moment (it necessarily had to be withdrawn from the conventional ceremonial lyric, for example, during coronation, a visit by the monarch, and so on), when the symbol of the ancient king, for example, had to be displaced by the official king—"you have become the seat of kings, as well!"[10] But it did enter into play quite often: from the beginning, monuments of the magnificent Czech past have been perceived from this melancholic perspective, even where it did not seem logical. As early as František Turinský's historical drama,* whose present tense is precisely that adored glorious past, the particularly Revivalist view of the past was preserved: "in the castle—crown of the fatherland / . . . where the Czech strings blissfully resounded, / here it is empty, as if the nation had died!"[11] Similar elements can be found in the historical prose of Josef Linda:† "It is desolate around Vyšehrad, sad within;—Within glorious, proud Vyšehrad . . . Where are those whom the nation honors? Where is thunderous Perûn?‡ . . . Where is the nation of the Slavs, where are the former times of the Slavs!"[12]

At the same time, however, Prague is—as a collection of emblems with a past sign and past values—a "holy place," a "sanctum," a space where this world meets "the other world," a reality with a sacred world of patriotic ideals. The manner in which Prague is incorporated into the Revivalist ideological system is like a restoration of ancient mythological thinking and its forms. The role of Prague in the classical Revivalist system in many respects recalls the functions of "the cosmic tree"—arbor mundi—and its equivalent, the mytheme of "the mountain" as a link between the world of people and the world of gods.[13] From this perspective, it is revealing that Prague is placed in "the center"—"a charming valley in the heart of Europe," the "center."[14] Similarly, Prague's objective aspect is above all as the bearer of reference to high values and retrospectively their mere reflection, which does not have any value in itself. It is a dead reality, "a mountain of rocks." Again, analogically, this reference was spatially oriented toward the function of the mythical mountain: It is a vector directed from below—from the objective—upward toward the ideal, in which only it was, from the perspective of Revivalist logic, the guarantee of the significance of the entire Czech world. "Castle," "towers," "ramparts," "cathedral," "throne," and "altar" are from this functionally generalizing perspective similar to the mountain.[15]

Here it may be appropriate to point out when the mountain is transformed into the national sanctum—Říp or Radhošť, Tatry, Blaník, and Krkonoše:

* František Turinský (1797–1852) was a dramatist of the National Revival. In 1848 authorities forbade the performance of his play *Pražané 1648*.

† Josef Linda (1792–1834) was a Czech writer. Together with Václav Hanka he is considered the author of the Zelenohorský and Královédvorský manuscripts. See chapter 2, "Mystification and the Nation."

‡ Perûn is the Slavic god of thunder and lightning.

TO THE RADOŠŤ MOUNTAIN IN MORAVIA

Thus the supreme *Slávie* stands!
The oceans foam beneath her *throne*
Eternally ruling, and her proud
Companions bow humbly before the sovereign:

Lofty Radošť *towers above*!
Shielding its venerable head in the clouds,
Shielding its foundations in the bowels of the Earth:
Thus she rules over the stately mountains . . .

Joyously, Radošť, claim your *crown*!
You *altar* of the Slavs and *Slavie*
You faithful *monument*! Your cheerful gaze
arouses bright happiness in the soul.

Welcoming clans no longer reek with the smoke
of their swarming victims; the hallowed grove
calls no longer even to glorious "Radogost!"
Temple and priest have grown mute on you forever;

Nonetheless, the *ancient* oak keeps
your faithful secret; and hard by a choir of forests
fallen ominously silent breathes the strength of the
departed fathers into the hearts of their progeny.

Thanks to you, intimate creator of the tender
dreams of my youth: my soul rushes to you
full of joy: allow me to live in the shadow
of your holiness, oh Noble One.

Here from the bustling springs I want to draw
the Slavic strength; and the awakened majestic
cliffs will spread far and wide the peculiar
sounds of my Slavic lyre.[16]

The mountain, which becomes a component of the National Revival myth, has an iconography similar to Prague. The metaphorics of the mountain are equally "architectonic" (cathedral, ramparts) just as the metaphorics of the city are "mountainous"; an analogous chain of attributes appears here—"crown," "throne," and "altar." The mountain is explicitly labeled as a sanctum, it soars upward ("shielding in the bowels of the Earth its own foundations"; "shielding its head in the clouds"), it is "ancient," and it is a place of contact with the past, primarily the mythological past ("sacred groves," "sacrifice," "the ancient oak"). In each case, it is a place of colloquy with the sanctum ("majestic cliffs"), with "departed fathers," a sign of a glorious past and its ideal timeless projection "of the supreme *Slávie*." It is possible to state without exaggeration that the image of Prague and the image of Radhošť from the previous example, the image of the city and mountain, is, from the perspective of the needs of the National Revival, at a certain level an entirely interchangeable generalization. In other words, the roles of both the "city" and the "mountain" as a national sanctum are essentially the same.

Of course, this does not mean that reality (if the process of the "sanctification" of a city or a mountain in one or another National Revival movement prevails) will be mere chance or the result of a patriotic group's free choice.[17] Although in principle the emblematics of both national sanctums are identical, the elevation of one of them over the other clearly reflects definite geographical and especially historical assumptions and therefore an entirely different situation of the Revivalist movement. In the end, however, it also offers other solutions for the future. From this perspective, the confrontation with its closest neighbors, with the Slovak National Revival, is exceptionally interesting. If Prague becomes for us the central component of the national myth, in Slovakia the mythicization of cities (Nitra, Bratislava) is peripheral. The fundamental national place of sanctification becomes the Tatra Mountains.

Even before the rise of the Ľudovít Štúr* generation, the Tatras become the symbol of Slovakia for Ján Hollý[†] (in his poem *Svätopluk*, Slovakia is referred to directly as Tatransko, and the Slovaks as Tatrans). And within the framework of mutual Czech-language culture, Ján Kollár[‡] glorifies the Tatras as the cradle of Slavs. However, the Štúr generation takes possession of the Tatras and transforms them into the cornerstone of their ideology with such enthusiasm that in a polemic with them, Kollár himself mounts an attack with peculiar mockery on the Tatra myth itself. The central geographic location of the Tatra Mountains

---

* Ľudovít Štúr (1815–56) was a Slovak politician, journalist, and linguist. He was the most notable advocate of Slovak nationalism during the nineteenth century.
† Ján Hollý (1785–1849) was a Slovak writer and translator.
‡ Ján Kollár (1793–1852) was a Slovak poet, prose writer, and Pan-Slavist. His most famous work, *Sláva dcery* (Daughter of Sláva, 1824), a cycle of Petrarchan sonnets glorifying the past of the Slavs and lamenting their present state, made him famous throughout the Slavic world.

alone spoke in favor of transforming them into a national Slovak sanctum. In Poland, by contrast, not even during times of heightened interest in the Tatras in the 1870s and '80s did the mountains achieve similar elevated status. For the Poles, they remained border mountains, the exotic and geographical periphery rather than an essential part of the homeland's image.[18]

The sanctification of the city in Slovakia was hindered not only, as in our case, by the present—that is, the present status of the estrangement of the city as a whole from national life and language—but also by the unsuitability of using the city as a sign for the complex of supreme values of the "great national past." The Slovak city—in contrast to the Czech city—did not call to mind any former independent national existence and was thus losing the prestige necessary for a Revivalist ideology. The Slovak city did not recall former national independent historical existence and was thus less prestigious.

The sanctification of the Tatras, by contrast, could become such a symbol. Even before the Štúr generation, the Tatras partially fulfilled this role as the "center and cradle" of the Slavic people. The Štúr generation merely codified and made absolute this semiotic function. Just as Prague became for Czech patriotic society a materialization of the former glorious historical existence of the Czech nation, the Tatras became for the Štúr Revivalist generation "the idea of Slovakia, petrified, embodied because that majesty and strength, that immense giant looking down upon you, evokes in the Slovak soul a somber sense of a great calling."[19]

Prague and the myth of the Tatras opened up different possibilities. The mythicization of Prague elevated the work of mere human hands to the level of sanctum, whereas the mythicization of the Tatras transformed a natural formation into a national sacrament a "work of God." Thus, the Slovak national movement became even more closely connected with the notion of being chosen by God. This became evidence that the nation was capable of receiving this task assigned by Providence. Another, more important factor was the fact that Prague, as a sanctum, was one that was inhabited. It was precisely Prague that was the actual center of everyday patriotic activity. Yet nothing alters the fact of how little of its reality entered into the consciousness of the National Revivalists, who saw Prague first and foremost as a simple complex of evaluatively arranged emblems. For the Slovak National Revival, the Tatras were a space that was uprooted from everyday life, a place of national patriotic ceremonies, but not of everyday patriotic work.[20] The literary appropriation of the image of Prague, which was in the 1830s and '40s already a battle for the appropriation of the conceptual scheme and which created a component of the overall realization of the Revivalist movement and the initial disintegration of actual Revivalist ideology itself, was at the same time facilitated by easy access to the sanctum. However, it appears that the very manner in which the image of the Tatras was drawn into the ideology of the Štúr generation had a clearly appellative character. The union with a divine calling became the bearer of an important moral imperative: let us be ready for the future deed. The consecration of Prague, by comparison, was a referring to the past: this is how we used to be.

Naturally, it is not possible to conclude from this that a historically, geographically, and socially conditioned choice of whichever national symbol would have then further influenced the behavior of the national collective. The choice did, however, provide the nation with a definite set of expressive means, which in the future were sometimes more suitable than at other times for individual national tasks. Sometimes they were extremely appropriate, sometimes they remained neutral, and sometimes they were at odds with the task and had to be reconstructed. Nevertheless, they could reflect characteristic features of this or that societal current, which would otherwise remain hidden.

The peculiarity of the image of Prague inheres in the city's duplex nature, in which Prague as the center of the national myth combines with Prague as an urban organism.[21] It was the result of combining the idea of the modern city with Revivalist ideology, which in our conception is Jungmann's ideology. In its origin, the Revivalist image of Prague as a sanctum did not suffer in any way by its fusion with reality. Jungmann's entire complex of emblems and their attributes remained an important element of envisioning Prague throughout the entirety of the nineteenth century—no matter how little it represented its own reality. Its extremely general character allowed relatively easy combination with new elements—even the mythical phantomlike metropolis at the turn of the century could not entirely interrupt intercourse with this layer of the image of Prague.[22] For a long time it fulfilled the National Revival function, which had still not been completely dissipated, whereby multifaceted reality joined the consecrated, a priori ideological and lucid reality of national values.

6

The Bridge

The Czechs have often seen their historical position as a "bridge" between the Slavs of the east and the Germans of the west. After Word War II, President Edvard Beneš sought to revive the image of Czechoslovakia as a bridge between the Communist East and the democratic West. He negotiated the removal of both Soviet and American troops from Czechoslovakia, which made Czechoslovakia unique among the countries defeated or liberated by either army.

I believe there is one nineteenth-century Czech dramatic work more viable than the rest. With a bit of exaggeration, one could say that this work points directly from its depths, where the modern Czech literary tradition was born, to Václav Havel's Absurd Theater. Perhaps only Bohuslav Martinů* noticed the qualities offered by this small dramatic text—nothing more than a one-act play, a mere farce—when he decided to use it as a model for his opera. Yes, I am talking about *Comedy on the Bridge* by Václav Kliment Klicpera.† The play's tone is neither nationalistically arousing nor patriotically militant. Its action is entirely abstract and does not offer idyllic reflections on national life. The play concerns two people stuck on an unnamed bridge above an unnamed river in an unnamed land. They are unable to cross over or return because soldiers of enemy armies have closed both sides of the bridge.

The theme, entirely free of the ideological pronouncements common at the time, is surprisingly stimulating; it seems to have something essential to say—perhaps about the banality of everyday human problems against the background

---

* Bohuslav Martinů (1890–1959) was a Czech composer. His most famous works are the opera *Juliet* (1938) and the orchestral work *Memorial to Lidice* (1943).
† Václav Kliment Klicpera (1792–1859) was a Czech playwright, prose writer, and poet. He was one of the founders of Czech drama and was especially influential in the foundation of comedic Czech theater. *Comedy on the Bridge* was written in 1826 and published in 1828. Martinů's variation, *Little Suite from Comedy on the Bridge*, had its premier in New York in 1935.

of historical events, or, on the contrary, about the nonsensicalness of historical mechanisms against the background of everyday human life. Or perhaps the theme is the bridge itself, the bridge as a symbol.

From the beginning of the formation of Czech national awareness, the notion of national identity was connected to this symbol. Just as the Russians have their emblem "a window to Europe," introduced by Peter the Great, and the Bulgarians speak of "a gate to Europe,"* the concept of Czech culture and the meaning of its national existence was identified with the image of a bridge connecting one world with another, one culture with another.

It is sufficient to recall how František Palacký† formulated the idea in his introduction to *The History of the Czech Nation in Bohemia and Moravia*. According to Palacký, the Czech nation was allotted the task of "serving as a bridge between the Germans and the Slavs and between the east and the west in Europe in general." This lofty notion faithfully accompanied the process of Czech national emancipation; it lived on even during the First Czechoslovak Republic. In the confusing postwar period before February 1948, this notion assumed a preservative value, which both resisted efforts to drag Czech culture and everything with it into the Eastern sphere, as well as distanced it from Western influences. Otherwise, and primarily, this notion bore witness to the significance of the Czech nation and its culture (whatever it may be); it provided its existence with a further dimension, which other nations might have seen as superfluous, perhaps even foolish, but it has always played an immense role in the Czech imagination, a metaphysical one. Czech national identity has never been satisfied with the type of pronouncement "we are"; it has always required a different declaration of identity: "we are, because we have a metaphysical mission."

To be a bridge seemed a sufficient justification; it added to the significance of the nation and its culture. At the same time, the creation of Czech culture as a complete and independent "Czech world" in all respects isolated it as well. It erected a barrier and a protective filter. The image of the bridge provided a counterweight to the necessity of enclosing oneself in one's own traditions, language, and themes, which always inherently accompany the formation of a new

---

* The Russians consider the city of Saint Petersburg a "window to Europe," and the Bulgarians refer to the city of Rousse as a "gate to Europe."
† František Palacký (1798–1876) was the founder of modern Czech historiography and a leading figure in the Czech National Revival. He advocated Czech autonomy within a strong Austrian Empire as the best protection against German and Russian pressure. *The History of the Czech Nation in Bohemia and Moravia* was published in five volumes beginning in 1848 until the year of his death.

national culture. This symbol also imparted a wider supranational dimension to the inner impulse of national emancipation, of the creation of modern Czech culture. We are because we are the intermediary of the meeting of two cultures, two worlds. We are perhaps even the foundation, or at least a condition, for a future synthesis of these two valuational regions.

It seems today that little remains of this image. Its lofty self-assurance did not suit the plans of even the most ardent apostles of the new postwar era. Every attempt to resurrect this traditional Czech ideogram was stridently rejected from the left. Our duty was not to become a bridge between East and West, but rather a stalwart constituent of the new socialist world, its "embankment," "cape," "shield"—not to be the region of a fertile meeting of values, but a bulwark against the penetration of all things foreign from the West.

If that ancient symbol does appear sometimes even now, it is unrecognizable in its extreme modesty. When at the end of the Normalization era Milan Uhde* began publishing a new literary journal titled *The Bridge etc.*, he had in mind a bridge that was to span the artificial (yet deep) rift within Czech culture itself. His intention was a matter of crossing at least internal borders: "The boundaries between those who left Czechoslovakia and those who stayed. The boundaries between those who are not permitted to publish and those who are." Another recently established journal, *Bridges*, returns to the same symbol in an attempt to cross the border between Slovaks and Czechs.

In both cases, a worldwide or all-European bridge became essentially a construction of only regional importance. We are striving to connect only ourselves. The distant National Revival symbol has been reduced to realistic boundaries. It is as if Klicpera anticipated this development in his farce. It seems only appropriate that *Comedy on the Bridge* be performed today.

---

* Milan Uhde (b. 1936) is a Czech playwright and politician. He became a dissident during the Communist years, and after the Velvet Revolution he accepted the post of Minister of Culture and head of the Chamber of Deputies.

PART II

The Joyous Age

Reflections on Czechoslovak Communism

7

The Potato Bug

In response to the Korean War, the Czechoslovak government began an anti-America propaganda campaign by accusing American "gangsters in airplanes" of deliberately airlifting the potato bug to Socialist potato fields to destroy their crops. Dropping this exotic insect, which originated in the United States, from their planes in boxes and bottles resulted in the sabotage of the Czechoslovak people's hard work. The potato bug, also referred to as "the six-legged ambassador of Wall Street," became a symbol of imperialistic designs on the countries of Socialism. Soviet pilots came to the rescue and sprayed the affected fields with pesticide. Just as they did during World War II, they helped their neighbor prevail.

Before the war, the French intellectual Roger Caillois examined the unusually powerful impact a certain specimen of the insect kingdom had on the human imagination, that is, the praying mantis, and he devoted an extensive section of his book *Le mythe et l'homme* (Myth and Mankind) (1938) to the mantis and the myth. Caillois could not have suspected that a dozen years later an entirely different type of insect would capture the imagination of someone in Eastern Europe, an insect that at first glance appears much less astounding, a diminutive member of the order *Coleoptera* and the family *Chrysomelidae*—a shapely, squat bug with dark yellow striped wings and a dark, spotted yellow carapace. It was certainly an exotic insect, originating in North America, and it did, after all, present in one way or another a genuine threat to the production of potatoes. Nevertheless, the degree of its collective demonization was extraordinary.

On 28 June 1950 the government of the Czechoslovak Republic issued a proclamation to its citizens, which was picked up the very next day by every Czechoslovak daily news outlet. The proclamation began with a dramatic contrast:

> Every day our working class farmers—and, along with them, the entire nation—
> oversee the ripening of the grain and the harvesting of the crops with the joyful hope
> and care of conscientious tillers of the soil. They work in unison with the heartfelt

and industrious participation of our entire nation toward the second harvest of the five-year plan. And precisely at the moment joyful preparations are underway to begin harvesting the fruit of the yearlong constructive work of our small- and medium-scale farmers, news is arriving from the western and southwestern parts of our republic concerning a serious threat to this year's potato crop by the potato bug.

In past years, this villainous potato-crop saboteur appeared in a small number of our villages. The concentrated efforts of farmers, youths, citizens and the People's Administration of the afflicted villages along with the efforts of research workers succeeded in gradually localizing and finally liquidating the harmful parasite. With the help of abundant Soviet experience in anti-potato-bug battle and with the willing, brotherly participation of Soviet experts over several years, last year the threat of the potato bug was effectively overcome.

This year over the course of a few days, the potato bug has suddenly and on a massive scale laid low all the western and southwestern regions of the republic bordering the occupied zones of Western Germany. From there, the potato bug is spreading throughout the nation. In the western regions of the country, the potato bug has appeared not only in the fields, but also in town squares, streets, and backyards. In several districts, the potato bug has been found primarily near roads and highways. Boxes and bottles have also been found filled with this beetle. All of this is irrefutable evidence that the present potato bug peril did not arise, and could not have arisen, through natural and normal routes. This dangerous parasite was transported to us artificially, intentionally, and on a massive scale with the assistance of the clouds and winds of Western imperialists and their agents and saboteurs sent to dwell among us.

In the proclamation, this "reality" was further designated as an "unprecedented attack on the livelihood of our farmers," and the government expressed its conviction that "our working people would reject with disgust and revulsion this criminal attempt to destroy the harvest and would annihilate the perpetrators before the eyes of the entire civilized world. The people would see to it that the attempt would end in utter failure by responding with a massive and decisive battle against the potato bug, which had been unlawfully and viciously transported to us. They would reveal the true face of the imperialists and war mongers, along with their malignant agents."[1]

The potato bug immediately became the impetus for the issuance of diplomatic communications. On 2 July 1950 the Soviet government sent the U.S. government a letter accusing the American side of sabotaging the fields of the German Democratic Republic. A week later, the Czechoslovak government sent a letter to the American embassy in Czechoslovakia.

The timing of the entire campaign itself was noteworthy. The anti–potato bug proclamation appeared in newspapers two days after the announcement of the outbreak of the Korean War, that is (in the official version) after "the American puppet government of South Korea initiated an armed attack against the Democratic People's Republic of Korea."[2]

The potato bug case was consistently associated with the Korean War, and the two topics often appeared side by side: "While the air assassins of the American Air Force drop bombs on residential areas of Korean cities, not even Europe has been spared the 'pacificatory deeds' of the American imperialists."[3] "The members of the Standard Farming Cooperative in Jednomělice in the district of Slaný protest the assault against the Democratic People's Republic of Korea. We have declared war throughout the community against the potato bug, which is being transported to our area by abettors of hawks and warmongers. . . . We find clear evidence of this in the criminal assault on the Democratic People's Republic of Korea and the subversive dropping of the potato bug into the regions neighboring the German/American occupation zone."[4] The humor magazine *Dikobraz* presented an anecdotal conversation between two American pilots: "So, are we dropping bombs on Korea?" "No, the potato bug on Europe."[5]

This close relationship finally emerged in the tendency to stylize texts on the potato bug using wartime terminology. The previously cited proclamation initiating the campaign distinctly recalls an appeal to citizens after an unforeseen military attack. It juxtaposes a comforting scene of joyful, peaceful work with a dark portrayal of threat. It emphasizes the arrival of danger from the western border and summons the "people" to confront it head on. Even the terminology employed seems to come from a military dictionary—"engagement" or even "massive engagement," "localize and ultimately destroy," "overcome," "capture," "attack," and so on.

With this in mind, let us place two completely different texts side by side. Zikmund Skyba in an article titled "Gangsters in Airplanes," for example, even borrows the genre outline of the government's "call to arms": "Suddenly during the joyful and peaceful harvest preparations, voices sounded the alarm. . . . Attention, citizens of the Republic! This most beautiful land of yours has been attacked by the potato bug." The author then assumes the role of wartime correspondent and announces that "the battle against the saboteur has begun on the widest front, and means have been mobilized, which are proving their worth. We have entered into a battle that we must win at all costs."[6]

One would expect that a text from the children's section of a newspaper—for the moment we shall remain with *Lidové noviny*, with their traditional section intended for Young Pioneers—would offer a rather different mode of verbal expression and afford a certain alteration within the scope of the given topic. We discover, however, that this is not the case. In a story by Jíra Hodka, characteristically titled "Into Battle with the Enemy," young Vašek discovers a potato bug and goes to inform the chairman of the People's Council. The chairman decides, once again characteristically: "We must immediately mobilize all children from eight to fourteen years of age, along with their teachers." Further on, the text varies little and, despite its formal literary character, remains within the framework of a wartime news broadcast: "In an instant, the formation of warriors launched into relentless battle. . . . By evening, the potatoes were saved and the further spread forestalled of this terrible saboteur transmitted by America. The enemy was utterly defeated."[7]

Against this backdrop, the potato bug could not possibly be a mere potato bug. It became an adversary, the enemy of a people stalwartly constructing their Socialist country ("Our tables will not be safe until we exterminate the last potato bug. And the world will not breathe a sigh of relief until the last enemy of peace is neutralized"[8]). The potato bug was immediately transformed into a symbol, an emblematic animal of the West. Its characteristics seemed to express the fundamental characteristics of imperialists, primarily, of course, North American imperialists. "The parasites of Wall Street have called upon parasites from the insect world for help," declared *Rudé právo* on 30 June 1950.[9] Similar sentiments were expressed in verse by Karel Bradáč ("The parasitical insect has insect allies"[10]) and Václav Lacina:

A crisis is looming over Capitol Hill
where Mr. Dollar meditates on war
and wonders whom to send into the field:
Find him—it's difficult to go oneself, he's afraid.

He would shatter his sword against the iron shield,
The wickedest of weapons is not foreign to him:
The pestilence itself seeks to exterminate us with pestilence.
The insect himself sends to us his fellow insects.[11]

An important sign that linguistically connected the contemporary mythology of the potato bug with American imperialism was its "voracity" ("its voracity also recalls imperialism"; "We will not let a single grain, a single potato be destroyed by this voracious beetle whose features so much resemble those who sowed it among us"[12]). Subsequently, further characteristics of the beetle entered the game—visual characteristics, for example, which are so beloved in political caricatures and illustrations. The lengthwise stripes on the potato bug's carapace elicited comparisons with the American flag. In a drawing by Antonín Pelc, for example, we see a working-class fist crushing the center of a nest of potato bugs, while some, bearing human faces and sporting the tell-tale accessories—a Western top hat, a general's cap—are fleeing in fright. One of the bugs, an obvious caricature of then U.S. President Harry Truman, has a carapace in the form of the U.S. flag.[13]

At the same time, the potato bug not only symbolized imperialists (American imperialists), but it was also, in contemporary thinking, their tool. According to the need, the bug symbolized variously "the vicious seed sown by the imperialists,"[14] some sort of grotesque, inverted image of postwar UN parcels,[15] but metaphorically they were also obedient imperialist henchmen: "Americans are not ashamed to ally themselves with traitors, murderers, Nazi cutthroats, and collaborators. The potato bug is a new ally of the imperialists."[16] "Oh, were they to succeed in destroying all of our potato crops! Then they would rejoice: We have fulfilled the task assigned to us by the masters of the West."[17]

The potato bug became a symbol for all so-called enemies of Socialism at home, beginning with Josip Tito* and ending with Záviš Kalandra,† who were seen likewise as "vicious seeds" sown in the countries of Eastern Europe: "The introduction of the potato bug into our fields," writes the daily *Rudé právo*, "is merely a further link in the chain of provocation by American imperialists, the chain that leads from the planting of agents such as Tito, László Rajk,‡ and Trajčo Kostov§ in the lands of the people's democracy . . . to the support of spies and traitors in Czechoslovakia such as Horáková** and her accomplices."[18]

* Josip Tito (1892–1980) was the Communist president of Yugoslavia (1953–80). He broke with Stalin in 1948 and freed Yugoslavia from the control of the Soviet Union. It became the most liberal Communist nation in Europe.

† Záviš Kalandra (1902–50) was a prominent Czech Communist journalist who broke with the party over the Moscow show trials. He is alleged to have written a famous anti-Stalinist manifesto titled "We Protest!" He was hanged in June 1950 for treason and espionage.

‡ László Rajk (1909–49) was Minister of the Interior and Minister of Foreign Affairs in the Hungarian Communist Party. He was arrested and executed in a show trial for being a "Titoist spy."

§ Trajčo Kostov (1897–1949) was general secretary of the Bulgarian Communist Party from 1946 to 1949. In a show trial he was tried and executed for anti-Soviet propaganda and activity.

**Milada Horáková (1901–50), a Czechoslovak Parliamentary deputy, was tried and executed for treason and espionage. Her trial aroused worldwide protests and appeals for clemency from, among others, Albert Einstein.

It was no accident that Josef Kainar in his poem "Plot of Land" (the title itself
is revealing)—a literary affirmation of the verdict passed on Rudolf Slánský*
and his "accomplices"—condemns the "traitor" with a metaphor whose background is probably unclear to today's reader. A contemporary of Kainar's, however, could not but have perceived an obvious reference to the baleful image of
the potato bug: "Only treachery flies to us / upon the western winds."[19] After all,
this very motif formed a firm component of the "American beetle" myth, "the
six-legged ambassador of Wall Street," hurled allegedly from airplanes "into the
storm clouds and winds wafting from west to east."[20]

At the time, the image of the world was sharply polarized, divided into irreconcilable opposites: on one side was us, on the other them; on one side the East,
and on the other the West; at one pole the Kremlin, and at the other Wall Street;
heaven on one side, hell on the other; good versus evil; peace versus war. The
potato bug catastrophe that took place on our territory inevitably accommodated itself to this polarity. The potato bug was seen as a foreign enemy element.
It was designated as the American beetle, that is, as an invader, not only linked to
America by its origin, but simultaneously representing that "world of evil," which
extended westward from our border. The potato bug allowed us to refer to it as
"the insect world." The fact that the potato bug itself (especially in pictorial manifestations) was anthropomorphized with the help of well-established attributes
characterizing then-current perceptions of capitalism allowed the West to be
caricatured and relegated to the grotesque realm of contemptible animalistic
creatures. To be sure, this was perhaps a dangerous and certainly repulsive realm,
but at the same time, one undoubtedly doomed to extinction:

> Potato bugs and roaches, this is it,
> Invade our fields and try to cross our fences.
> No matter what, you'll end up in the sh—.
> I really meant to say, that is, our trenches.[21]

This, however, sometimes concealed the fundamental motif in the repertoire of
texts concerning the potato bug, which were anchored, as we have seen, in the sty-
listic register of war and contained new elements referring to the motifs of modern Socialist celebration. Its fundamental outlines, for the most part, crystallized

---

* Rudolf Slánský (1901–52), former general secretary of the Czechoslovak Communist Party,
  was at the center of the most spectacular of the Stalinist show trials of the 1950s, in which he
  along with thirteen others were charged with treason. Slánský was hanged in 1952.

around the framework of demonstrations and processions or the ostentatious ceremonial setting of collective construction. The battle against the potato bug is usually understood (and we see this most clearly once again in pictorial representations) as a celebration: Ondřej Sekora placed on the back cover of his agitprop brochure a procession of children armed with jars and bottles to capture the insects and added the caption "Everyone into battle against the potato bug." Lev Haas was acting in the same vein when he authored a political cartoon with the caption "The entire nation into battle against the American beetle!" A throng of people is depicted in the right half of the cartoon, half of whom are moving in a skirmish line and half in an organized procession. A truck driving in front of the crowd resembles a parade float and bears a prominent sign that reads more like a battle slogan.[22]

The potato bug was—at least for a portion of the year—part of a generally obligatory ceremony: The collection and destruction of the potato bug assumed the character of a noble task ("All you young pioneers form a line / Catch it, kill it, it's the potato bug!"[23]). It was a stimulus for proclaiming work obligations (F. Svoboda from Bretnov na Bruntálsku, in response to the potato bug danger, commits himself to fulfilling his potato purchasing quota 130 percent[24]) and for ritualized reports (in a poem by J. Červený titled "A Letter for Comrade Gottwald," a girl informs the president of the republic of her participation in an anti–potato bug campaign).

The unwelcome presence of the "American beetle" in Czech potato fields was actually a welcome ideological controversy. It confirmed the logic of dividing the world into the world of honorable labor, crowned with a rich harvest, and the insane world of values gone awry, in which "the Americans cultivated the potato bug to destroy crops."[25] The potato bug affair helped bring to a head the irreconcilable division of the world. At one pole was the American plane dropping bombs on Korea and the "vicious seed" of the agricultural parasite on us. At the opposite pole, Soviet planes were bringing help with chemical treatment of cooperative fields.

Let us return once more to the extensively cited government proclamation. From the very beginning, the campaign was accompanied by fervent thanksgiving to the Soviet Union for its assistance. The proclamation was reflected in fantastic news reports about the attempts of selfless Soviet scientists to cultivate a potato that was inedible for the potato bug.[26] The reports primarily concerned, however, the staunch and successful activity of Soviet pilots flying over affected areas, which was repeated in numerous articles and feuilletons. In the given propaganda register, it was an easy matter for Soviet pilots to stand out as the

"About the Mean Potato Beetle." Artist: Ondřej Sekora. This illustration appeared on the cover of a children's propaganda book of the same name published by the government-owned Státní nakladatelství dětské knihy in 1950. Below the title, the text reads: "About the American Beetle Who Wants to Steal from Our Plates."

positive counterpart to the evil American pilots, as the "true fighters for peace," "the heroes of love and assistance."[27]

With the theme of Soviet pilots, the motif of the recent Soviet victory in World War II was brought to the fore. The direct participation of this or that Soviet pilot in the liberation of Czechoslovakia was among the most popular motifs. This was significant because the "American beetle" was often demonized and linked to fascism. It was designated, for example, as the "secret weapon" of imperialism. The marks on its carapace in professional descriptions were often seen as the outline of the letter V, which was associated with Hitler's wartime V (*Fau*) rocket campaign. But it was still more important for the uniform evaluation of "American imperialism" as a new version of fascism, and this was a mandatory element of the propagandistic language of the 1950s (see, for example, the "American *gauleiter* Eisenhower," the "American Gestapo"[28]). The alliance with the Soviet Union, which was victorious in World War II, became the guarantee of all victories to come. The campaign against the potato bug was their joyous promise.

8

Death of the Leader

The death of Josef Stalin in March 1953 and Klement Gottwald shortly thereafter stunned the Socialist world. Death, which was connected with the capitalistic West, was not compatible with the ideal world of the Communist East. Thus, the demise of both statesmen had to be abolished at least symbolically. Both leaders were embalmed and placed on display, thereby preserving them for the ages and proving immortality in the Socialist lands. Moreover, Gottwald's premature death was explained as faithfulness to Stalin, strengthening the bond between the two countries.

The semiotics of paradise necessitated the denial of death. Death appeared as something entirely unnatural, fundamentally disrupting the basic principles of the "new era." Socialism was, in its symptomatically eschatological conception, seen as the final achievement of an ideal realm of happiness and earthly bliss, and the natural fact of death came into sharp conflict with this notion. Death was thus semiotically divorced from the world of Socialism and connected with the foreign, unfriendly world beyond the borders of Eden. And just as death seemed "atypical" for the world of Socialism, it was seen as "typical" for the world of the capitalistic West (even the semantics of "east" as the place where the sun "is born" and "west," where it "dies," contributed to this view). According to the theory of the regular historical alternation of epochs, the West was already condemned to destruction by the emergence of Socialism—it was withering away and, in fact, already dead.

Within the Socialist world, death was connected with those who had broken away from the rest of society and were designated as "enemies," "traitors," and "hirelings of the West." They were representatives of the foreign "civilization of death"; they "sowed their seeds of death" in paradise and were themselves in return condemned to death.[1] Thus, the authorities were essentially merely completing the mythical schema: we equal life; they equal death.

If "death" was linked to some element of the Socialist world, the fundamental semantic tendency was toward a strict delimitation of its effectiveness. Death was understood as a result of external intervention, as a seed from the world of evil. In other words, the actual unnaturalness of death under Socialism necessarily led to the privileging of *unnatural* death, that is, violent death, which would be explained in various "stories" created by Socialist culture—for example, someone dying at the hands of the enemy. In any case, death in this interpretation demanded a special framework to shift it toward a positive assessment. Even a heroic death, one redeemed by a suprapersonal mission and thus one contributing to the favorable development of humankind, was weakened and in extreme cases could even lead to the creation of other, optimistic versions of traditional tragic events:

If Jan Hus* entered the Bethlehem Chapel† today
to preach the word of truth to his descendants,
what is Constance today?—No, he would not go there today
without many a Czech lowering his head,
It is to You, Gottwald, that Hus would render his appreciation.[2]

If death could not be excluded literally from the horizon, at least it had to be deprived of its tragic nature. If it resisted heroism, it had to be presented as an accidental personal incident wrapped in and concealed by universal values, which in principle it could not disturb because theses values were eternally alive.

As pointed out earlier, after World War II and especially after February 1948,‡ Klement Gottwald became one such universal sovereign value by means of a rapid process of mythologization. He became transcendental himself, and everything else was seen as a particular concretization or manifestation of his transcendental being ("Gottwald's nation," "Gottwald's party," "Gottwald's youth"). Even genuine human acts were only the fulfillment of Gottwald's general acts ("When you assigned blame, it was as if he were assigning blame; when you praised something, it was as if comrade Gottwald were praising . . ."[3]). It was a process that fully—even if on a hierarchically lower level—repeated the mytho-poetic processions regarding Joseph Stalin. In the collective consciousness, Stalin

---

* Jan Hus (ca. 1369?–1415) was a Czech priest and religious reformer influenced by the writings of John Wycliffe. He attacked the abuses of the clergy and went into exile in the southern Bohemian city of Tábor, which later became the seat of the radical wing of the Hussite movement. Hus was burned at the stake as a heretic in 1415 in Constance.

† The Bethlehem Chapel in Prague was being rebuilt in the early 1950s in a major Communist propaganda stunt orchestrated by the Minister of Education, Zdeněk Nejedlý. It was thus a highly charged symbol.

‡ In February 1948 the Communist Party of Czechoslovakia staged a coup and seized total control of the state and society.

Stalin and the first Czechoslovak Communist president, Klement Gottwald, 1951 (photo by Schlesinger)

and Gottwald formed the fundamental spiritual substance, the *logos*, of the entirety of reality. All social, political, and even natural phenomena were seen only
as the "embodiment" of Stalin and/or Gottwald, as a trait derived from them
("Stalin is life"; "Stalin, / you are the sun, / the water / the air"[4]).

The death of Stalin on 5 March 1953 and Gottwald nine days later sent a shock
wave throughout the Socialist world. The metamorphosis of both personalities
into symbols and, at the same time, their permeation throughout reality as a whole
had already reached such a degree that everything around appeared as a mere
symbol derived from these primary symbols. If death was something essentially
incompatible with Socialism, the death of "universals" (the transcendental values)
was never even considered. Literally, all of Socialist reality was founded on them:
Death would endanger the very foundation of the cosmos. To accept the death of
both statesmen as a fact would mean accepting the fact of world's disintegration.

If the general denial of death was an important mechanism of the Socialist
world's internal control, then it was even more necessary to symbolically abolish
the death of the leader. The demise of both statesmen was perceived as something entirely impossible ("You are not dead, impossible, / it is not true at all";
"I cannot believe that / which is not possible"[5]). In the most varied texts, the
motif "he did not die, he continues to live" is repeated in different forms ("—He
did not die, Mother, right? /—No, little one. . . . Alive he is!"; "He did not die, he
lives again!"; "Don't say—he died . . . / Such a person does not die"[6]).

To be sure, the transformation of a personage into myth made death tantamount to a cosmic catastrophe, but precisely because it also divorced the symbol
of Gottwald and the symbol of Stalin from their actual human referents, it ren-
dered the entire process of invalidating death much simpler. Long before March
1953, the mythical equivalence of the leader and "the people," "us," became fixed
in the national consciousness, but not only because he came from "the people"
or because the government of "the people" was realized through him. The way
the symbol Gottwald or Stalin penetrated all of reality simply aimed at the absolute fusion of leader and masses: "He—that is us." For that reason "powerful old
Death"[7] had to meet with failure. Stalin and Gottwald long ago achieved immortality; their lives persisted in the lives of the people ("Stalin has died.—But eternally, forever, he will live in us!"[8]) or in an even more pointed formulation—the
life of the people could continue only in the life of their leaders: "Oh Mighty,
Glorious, Victorious—we have accepted from You, what You gave us with Your
Death—*You yourself*—and in You we will live on!"[9]

At the beginning of March 1953, both deaths elicited a twofold reaction:
consternation, first of all, that death could touch even unearthly, sacred beings;

and, second, it gave rise to the ritual concealment and denial of the fact of death, which was, of course, all the more forceful because death had struck the very foundation of the system. This dual reaction was also seen in the official cere-mony of Gottwald's funeral and the accompanying political campaign. On the one hand, the monumental ceremony underscored the tragedy, the catastrophic nature of the event, not only its deep impact on the life of the entire society, but also the personal and painful experience that affected each individual. On the other hand, it was precisely this monumentality that confirmed the permanence and imperturbability of the Socialist world, which continued to function even though its creator, its "leader" in his physical shape, had passed on. The ritual of the state funeral itself enabled one to shift to the background the moment of leave-taking with a concrete human individual and subsequently to foreground the state, that is, its machinery and ideology. This was unconditionally empha-sized at the time. Stalin's funeral, for example, took place without the participa-tion of the intimate friends and relatives of the deceased.

In Gottwald's case, it was generally pointed out in official commentaries that, just as in the case of Stalin, death in no way altered the leader's appearance ("Death has not changed the features of the beloved face that is so familiar to the entire world"; "Even now strength, assurance, and confidence in the success of the work he has undertaken radiates from the peaceful face unchanged by death"[10]). Moreover, this represented the symbol of "death's failure" in the face of the majesty of the leader and of Socialism. The usual ritual symbols of death and sorrow (the black flag flying above the castle, black veils covering windows and mirrors, Greek fires, and so on) were accompanied by conspicuous sym-bols of Socialism: red cloth on the walls of the Spanish Hall, red flowers, a five-pointed star behind the catafalque and even on Wenceslas Square by the National Museum ("the sign beneath which the great deceased Gottwald fought and emerged victorious"[11]). The entire organization of the funeral ceremony accen-tuated the most important ideological elements of the Socialist state. Emphasis was placed on friendship with the Soviet Union ("this is not only an act of mourning . . . it is a grand manifestation by a hundred million hearts of the loyal and eternal unity of our nations with those of the Soviet Union"[12]). The parade of military strength by the armed forces and people's militia on Letná Boule-vard became an expression demonstrating that the death of the statesman did not cripple socialism. Crowds numbering hundreds of thousands streamed past the catafalque and accompanied the body of the "Workers' President" on his last journey, thus confirming the mythological thesis of the leader who lives on in his people and of the people who live on in their leader. Finally, in an updated version of the Hussite tradition, the coffin was placed on Vítkov Hill* to the strains of Bedřich Smetana's "Tábor,"† thereby pointing to the ancient roots of the new order.

The placement of the dead into the National Monument on Vítkov Hill and the transformation of the building into a mausoleum was eventually the glorious climax of the ritual battle with death, which was unleashed in Czechoslovakia in March 1953. By this act, the shock of death was definitively eliminated. The physical vessel of the deceased was not allowed to disintegrate, but was preserved for the ages. The embalming of the deceased was associated with a foreign, exotic tradition, one that was not typical in Europe, and which decisively transformed its significance. As Boris Groys points out, the deceased was not clothed in the ritual garments of transition to another world and hidden away from the eyes of mortals, but quite the opposite.[13] Gottwald was placed in a display case and transformed into an exhibition: the new, modern mausoleum combined the functions of an Egyptian pyramid and a museum. The deceased statesman was simply placed on display as eternal, earthly proof of his immortality.

The entombing of Gottwald in a mausoleum, however, did not refer directly to the ancient oriental tradition; it was primarily a repetition of the mummification of Stalin and Lenin. Just as the placement of Stalin in the mausoleum on Red Square next to Lenin was a gesture completing Stalin's deification, Klement Gottwald's installation on Vítkov had a similar effect. With this act, Czechoslovakia's first "Workers' President" was in fact placed at the side of Lenin and Stalin and likewise raised (of course, only temporarily) to the status of a demigod.

From the very beginning, the death of Gottwald was perceived as "faithfulness to Stalin" ("faithful even in death / to your teacher!"[14]), as a confirmation of the invincible bond between Czechoslovakia and the Soviet Union ("In life, they brought us closer for eternity, / In death, they have united us for eternity"[15]). The mausoleum transformed forever Gottwald's death into a memorial to Gottwald's greatness, a memorial to the greatness of a new era and the indivisible

---

* A "Memorial of National Liberation" was completed in 1932 on Vítkov Hill in Prague, which was the site of the celebrated Hussite victory over Emperor Zikmund's invaders in July 1420. The site offers a panoramic view of the city, and the memorial itself consists of a statue of the Hussite leader Jan Žižka, a mausoleum, and the museum of "National Liberation."

† "Tábor" is the most dramatic movement of Bedřich Smetana's great symphonic poem *Má vlast* (My Homeland, 1879). The movement employs the melody of the Hussite hymn "Ye who are the soldiers of God."

friendship with the Soviet Union. The golden letters of the name of Stalin, which appeared beside those of Lenin in the Moscow mausoleum, just like the letters KG in the Prague mausoleum, were proof of the transformation of the people Dzhugashvili and Gottwald into symbols, thus bearing witness to the power of symbolism, which could protect even the human body, the physical "bearer of the symbol," against the inexorable laws of natural processes.

9

Symbol with a Human Face

Alexander Dubček (1921–92) served briefly as head of the Communist Party of Czechoslovakia in 1968. Dubček is primarily associated with the Prague Spring, during which he became the symbol of the reform movement, that is, of "Socialism with a human face." His face was the face of reform, and this characterization was revived after November 1989 as the Slovaks sought sovereignty from the Czechs.

Even people change into signs. Directly before our eyes, Alexander Dubček was transformed into a legend, a myth, and a symbol. The process of semiosis—a term coined by Charles William Morris, the founder of modern semiotics, to refer to the process of how signs come into existence—rejects or pushes into the background various personality traits and biographical details, while emphasizing and making full use of others.[1]

Dubček became primarily the symbol of the Prague Spring and Socialism with a human face, of the hopes of this period and their swift collapse. Thus, motifs representing ordinary human qualities and achievements are emphasized in Dubček's iconography. Václav Havel says: "I knew him as a pleasant, sincere, and unassuming man."[2] Roman Kováč notes: "Throughout his life he was an ordinary and plain-spoken man, which gave him enormous authority both at home and abroad."[3] Čestmír Císař responds almost identically: "His character was of a decent and honest man."[4] Dubček's merging with the emblem of Socialism with a human face naturally focused attention on his own face: "modest," "smiling," in other words "human" ("A Communist with a Human Face," as the title of a newspaper article proclaimed).

Of course, even when Dubček is presented as an exceptional persona, his exceptionality has nothing in common with the expected official superiority of a Communist boss. Instead, he is affectionately presented something along the lines of an athlete performing an astonishing athletic achievement: Dubček is (in the words of Bohumil Hrabal) "a delightful dandy,"[5] "whose lissome form dives into the pool" (Břetislav Rychlík nostalgically notes and adds: "We will have no other childhood than the one in which Saša Dubček dove in head first"[6]).

In the process of this semiosis, even conceivable rebukes directed at Dubček the politician become virtues. From this perspective, any criticism of Dubček's political weakness or indecision is proof of his "humanity." As early as 26 August 1968, the daily *Mladá fronta* writes that Dubček was slow in opposing the Stalinist wing of the Communist party, but adds that he was "a terrific person with a heart of gold."[7] This was not "a philosophical thinker," readily admits Ladislav Ťažký in Dubček's obituary.[8] "He was neither an original thinker nor a successful politician, and he was frequently on the losing side in political battles for power," states Zdeněk Mlynář.[9] And beneath all these layers, which Mlynář and Ťažký perceive as nonauthentic, one finds Dubček—The Man ("a remarkable man"). Even as a politician, Dubček inspired confidence "more with his human rather than political qualities." That which would have been a handicap for another politician was actually an advantage for Alexander Dubček, a positive quality of his politics, "politics with a human face."[10]

The emphasizing of the motif of ordinariness and humaneness, of course, in no way excludes even more manifest processes of mythicization. In the representational key of the Prague Spring, Dubček is its "most beautiful, successful, well-developed, and symbolic flower" (L. Ťažký). But he's much more than that. Since August 1968 Dubček has been linked directly to the powerful motif of Christ. The traditional kiss of Russian political etiquette becomes the kiss of Judas—across from Judas Brezhnev* stands Christ Dubček. The poet Vojtech Mihálik developed this image immediately after the invasion: "Modern Christ, is there anything left from those kisses? / Dubček on the mount called Olivet / is sweating blood." Čestmír Císař writes, "For ordinary people Dubček had a Messiah's charisma, the charisma of Jesus Christ or Jan Hus." Bohumil Hrabal, too, compares Alexander Dubček to Christ: Dubček's eyes were those of "Christ praying on the Olivet mountain," and he sees his head adorned with a halo.

The journey through life of the legendary first secretary of the Communist Party of Czechoslovakia during the reform period—and even after November 1989—is viewed against the backdrop of the stations of the cross. "Shortly after November 1989 Alexander's Hosanna! was still resounding. All too soon, however, one began to hear from various quarters, 'Crucify him!'" complains Ťažký.

---

* Leonid Ilych Brezhnev (1906–82) was general secretary of the Communist Party of the Soviet Union from 1964 to 1982. He ordered the Warsaw Pact invasion of Czechoslovakia in August 1968, ending the Prague Spring.

Of course, recently these traditional processes of Dubček's symbolization have acquired entirely new motifs. Dubček's tragic car accident,* his long drawn-out death, and his passing on the anniversary of the Bolshevik Revolution on 7 November 1992 became not only a sign of the definitive end of the 1968 reform ideals, but also of the demise of Czechoslovakia. The press noted the coincidence of the location of the automobile accident, Humpolec, in the Slovak part of Czechoslovakia, and the declaration of Slovak independence. (See headlines from the daily *Lidové noviny* from 2 September: "Slovak National Council Accepts Slovak Constitution," "Opposition Demands the Convening of a Special Meeting of Both Houses of Parliament," "Alexander Dubček Injured in Car Accident—In Critical Condition.") The parallel between the death of the politician and the prolonged agony of the federation was generally shared. Even the concluding ritual itself had to be understood in this way, when the coffin bearing Dubček's bodily remains, draped by the Czechoslovak national flag (not by the multicolored display of the Bratislava festivities, which were dominated by the Slovak national flag) were lowered into the ground.

At the same time, the obituaries and commentaries on Dubček's death revealed implacable battles and clashes of different semiosis scrambling for supremacy. The Christ myth was confronted with the Christian distrust of new messiahs. J. Orel, the press spokesman of KDU-ČSL,[†] states: "I believe that Alexander Dubček is now standing before God. We must pray for him, as we pray for everyone, that he pass that test."

Dubček as a symbol of the Federation[‡] clashed with Dubček as a symbol of Slovak identity. This clash was expressed both by the anonymous Czech voices demanding Dubček's release from Czech medical care, "since they don't like us in Slovakia, anyway," and the numerous voices from Slovakia. Ľudovít Čermák, for example, called Dubček "the Slovak of our modern era." Naturally, even the "Pragocentric" term Prague Spring, poignantly associated with the Prague music festival of the same name, was frequently replaced by political neologisms that were perhaps more impartial. However, they were flat, lifeless, and rarely used: the Czech and Slovak Spring or the Prague and Bratislava Spring.

---

* Dubček died due to injuries sustained in a mysterious automobile accident on 1 September 1992. He was supposed to serve as a witness against several officers of the KGB a week after his death. Czechoslovakia split into the Czech and Slovak Republics on 1 January 1993.
† KDU-ČSL: The Czech Christian Democrats.
‡ In 1969 Czechoslovakia became a federation of the Czech Socialist Republic and Slovak Socialist Republic.

Dubček's death also became the sign of uniquely Slovak suffering and the archetypal Slovak "political fate." According to Ťažký, Dubček "shattered into countless pieces (!), just like the darling of the Slovak nation General Dr. Milan Rastislav Štefánik,[*] he was critically injured like Ľudovít Štúr,"[†] he was severed from his people by a violent death like Vladimír Clementis,[‡] Rudolf Viest,[§] Ján Golian,[**] and even the president of the Slovak state, Jozef Tiso[††] (against whom Dubček fought during the Slovak National Uprising). Furthermore, the topos of the stations of the cross became unambiguously Slovakized. In the Moravian Corridor beneath the inscription "Dubček's Last Station of the Cross" were photographs documenting the politician's journey through life arranged in the image of the Slovak two-barred cross. The crossbar consisted of three photographs: Dubček with Brežněv, the wrecked automobile by the highway, and Dubček with Havel.

Zdeněk Mlynář is correct in his reflections on Dubček's death: "It is possible to kill a man but not a symbol." Indeed, a symbol cannot be killed. A symbol can only be interpreted in various ways.

---

[*] Milan Rastislav Štefánik (1880–1919) was a Slovak diplomat, politician, and astronomer who helped found Czechoslovakia in 1918. He died in an airplane crash, the cause of which is still disputed.

[†] Ľudovít Štúr (1815–56) was a leader of the Slovak National Revival in the nineteenth century. A self-inflicted gunshot wound led to his death.

[‡] Vladimír Clementis (1902–52) was a Slovak politician. He was convicted on charges of treason and espionage in a show trial and hanged along with Rudolf Slánský.

[§] Rudolf Viest (1890–1945) was a Czechoslovak general and commander of the partisan army during the Slovak National Uprising. During the uprising he was captured, taken to Germany, and executed in a concentration camp.

[**] Ján Golian (1906–45) was a Slovak general and commander-in-chief of the Slovak Army during the Slovak National Uprising. He was captured and executed along with Rudolf Viest.

[††] Jozef Tiso (1887–1947) was a Slovak politician and Fascist President of the puppet Slovak state during World War II. After the war, he was convicted and hanged as a war criminal.

10

The Metro

The Prague metro system, built in the early 1970s, was more than merely a much-needed system of transport. It represented the ideal world of Socialist Czechoslovakia, which had overcome the "crisis" at the end of the 1960s (the Prague Spring). It was presented as a product of modern technology and as a structure of extraordinary societal significance. However, because Prague was the forty-third city in the world to build an underground transit system, it was not possible for the Czechoslovak government to insist on the metro's technological uniqueness. Only the complicated tunneling beneath the Vltava River, made possible by the Soviet tunneling shield, could be mythologized. In a propaganda film made at the time, a Soviet specialist who assists with the tunneling is depicted as leading a battle in Prague just as he did thirty years ago in May 1945. To link the metro with the Soviet Union's liberation further, many stations' names referred to various World War II battles (Dukelská and Sokolovská and evoked friendship with the Soviets—Moskevská and Družby). Given that only a few designations referred to the aboveground locality in Prague, the topography of the city seemed less important than the ideological evocation of the Soviet Union.

The metro occupies a new reality within the realm of the city, a reality that, due to its own system of coordinates, is distinctly located "beneath." The direction downward is certainly not semiotically unambiguous. It can be associated with such meanings as a direction toward the foundation, to the root, to certainties, or it can be linked with the image of contemplativeness, meditation.[1] Yet it is precisely this semantic sphere that is annulled by the basic function of the metro: Descending into the depths is in this case consistently linked with the elimination of a state of calm. Here, the bowels of the earth do not represent a refuge but rather a sanctuary of speed and transfer. Thus instead, the underground evokes disturbing associations: mystery, inaccessibility, the "other world," the "underworld," and the "realm of shadows." As a construction in the "underground," the metro necessarily displays elements of abnormality. It is an attempt to seize control of a realm that is essentially "inhuman" and in which different rules apply—

different distances and a different sense of time. The metro does indeed generate its own microcosm within the sphere of the city, but it ultimately loses all connection with it. It is an isolated world in which one remains apart, severed from one's bonds. This opens up all possible complications when sojourning in the underground. Moreover, there are no impulses to establish other bonds. Of course, the usual images of overcoming distance—which one finds in trains, boats, and airplanes—are not connected with underground travel, which is natural. The metro is a means of mass public transportation, but in comparison with other means of city transit, it is conspicuous for the weakening of its bonds to the image of traveling only from one end of the city to another. The isolation space of the metro is such that within it the route is abstracted, formalized. Instead, the metro resembles a sort of peristalsis, the endless pulsation of an intestine. It is not a region of travel, but rather a region of disappearance and reappearance in two opposite but equivalent directions. In a word, it is a "vanishing."

If we assume that literature, especially poetry, is a heightened sensitivity to the semiotic process, we need only consider from this point of view the topos of the metro among contemporary Czech poets. We shall soon see that it is in poetry that these semiotic spheres are most often actualized. The isolation of the metro from the surrounding world, its artificiality, is perceived clearly: "The Prague underground expels you from the season."[2] People also lose their interconnectedness in the underground. Primarily, they are transformed into a crowd, an anonymous mass.[3] The metro is a region of partings, losses, and disappearance: "I found myself at one of the metro stations / Where we intersect / Two tracks: / A—like alienation / C—like a *circulus vitiosus*."[4] Here, the individual loses his or her identity. A favorite motif in metro poetry is the menacing scene of meeting oneself, of doubling. A common element is escalators that hurl people toward one another (without allowing any contact) ascending and descending. Or the glittering glass of the cars: "I observe this passing embankment, / as if I were staring wistfully into a mirror"; "When I meet myself / in the metro twice daily . . ."[5] The underground is seen as close to the depths, and as a place for meditation it is perceived in an unambiguously grotesque light.[6] Downward means primarily toward the underworld and the myth of Orpheus: "I shall repeat this ancient dim-witted mistake / And glance back . . . / Eurydice!"[7] This myth finds its way into poets' verses even if they consciously reject the image: "The escalators of lines A and C / do not transport benumbed shadows to the underworld."[8]

The metro creates the tension in the opposition above and below, light and darkness. Especially the aforementioned composition—which is understood as

an Orphic wandering through the labyrinth of the underground rail system—
plays out these semantics to their extreme, and concludes with the theme of a girl
named Lucy, lost Eurydice's counterpart ("Then I heard someone utter your
name / Derived from light: / Lucie* . . ."[9]).

It is significant that even "speed," one of the technical virtues of the metro,
is seen as utterly unproblematic, perhaps only in children's poetry ("The metro
zips us along without a pause"; "The metro zips along in the bowels"[10]). There is
something ghostly in the speed of the underground ("The trains of the metro
went blind long ago / like ponies in the mines / over and over they collapse into
the harness . . ."[11]). Speed is always marked by its enclosure within a corridor and
thereby free from connotations ordinarily attached to trains (freedom, indomit-
ability, and so on). Its metaphorics are identified with images of oppressive
space—the eye of a needle ("I observe the final wagon of your locomotive / Disappearing / In the tunnel's darkness like yesterday / Into the eye of a needle"[12]),
rifle barrels ("projectiles of cars fired from the tube of Gottwald Bridge"[13]), a
sleeve ("The train pulls on the sleeve of darkness"[14]), and so on. Moreover, the
motif of speed is often engulfed by the metaphorics of oppressive space: "Like
in a metro, you wait your whole life in a tunnel, in the long strip of kilometers /
until they rip you out with an oxyacetylene torch / You are in a vault from which
the arms and legs of the living protrude."[15]

Theses semiotic fields associated with the metro are manifestly disturbing,
reviving age-old archetypes and entering into relationships with ancient myths,
which seem somehow inappropriate for people living at the end of the second
millennium. From the point of view of the metro's conception, they are doubtlessly undesired and arise independently. How does the project of the metro
itself counter this type of semiosis, which was to some degree to be expected? Let
us take at random one of the exceptionally moderate and relevant formulations
of the stated goal of the construction: "The philosophy of the conception of all
Prague metro stations, both above and below ground, is a single, unifying idea:
the progressive and technically flawless transportation structure will provide
the inhabitants of Prague with a harmonious, high-quality environment leading
in all directions and corresponding to the enormous societal import this structure undeniably occupies. It will thereby become a major factor in raising the
population's living standard."[16] This brief statement clearly foregrounds at least
two aspects of the metro: (1) the metro is a product of modern technology, and
(2) the metro is a structure of extraordinary societal significance.

---

* Lucie is from the Roman Lucius, from lux, "light."

The possibility, however, of countering this ancient myth of the underworld with the modern optimistic myth of technology, which emerged in the nineteenth century ("our age . . . walks along via steam"; "we gallop via steam"[17]), is extremely weak in the second half of the twentieth century. The locomotive was easily monumentalized when it appeared in the Czech lands 150 years ago. J. M. Hurban describes his first encounter with the railroad:

> The steam engine began to move, then suddenly took off and with a thundering roar sped like an arrow through the delightful plains. After a few moments we were breaking away from the elements themselves. . . . It seemed that reason was leading us directly to God, transporting us up to the heavenly heights. This enormous weight, this extensive line of cars, this great number of people, this fantastic burden was being pulled by simple, ordinary steam. Here we have those old legends and tales of our Slovak people about the great speed of Šemík, Tátoš,* the Wicked Witch, and so on ushered into reality by reason. The divine idea of speed entrusted to human reason is now realized by human reason. As reason flies across the wide expanse of industry, art, and science, incessantly discovering new realms, so was the steam engine—the product and the invention—flying with us through the Austrian countryside.[18]

Somewhat later, Pravoslav Trojan Knovízský recorded his impressions on the arrival of the first train to Prague: "The steam engine surging mightily along the foot of Žižkov Hill . . . slowed its run like a champion and proceeded with long, majestic strides to halt at one of the new gates, that is, at the threshold of our Prague."[19] Finally, the Moravian Karel Šmídek, inspired by his encounter with the railroad, was moved to remark in a philosophic vein:

> I left this majestic theater moved to the utmost. Once again the truth was confirmed for me that humanity, like an unleashed torrent, is always rushing forward. Life always provides the mind and science with impulses to new and fresh activity. Neither the mind nor science can slacken wherever this internal element is to be found. This limitless fount of infinite depth will never be exhausted! Ever new efforts and ever new transformations are in the offing, and we will never reach the end! The spirit creates in eternal striving. Science and ingenuity are limitless; neither belongs to any age; their transformations will endure as long as humanity.[20]

---

* Šemík and Tátoš are horses from Czech and Slovak fairy tales.

This enchanted view of technology, however, belongs irretrievably to the past. In the nineteenth century, modern means of transport could successfully vie with chthonic forces because according to the contemporary mindset, they were on the same level: both were improbable and miraculous. Today, however, the railroad is simply one more innovation. Moreover, the metro system was an innovation only from a local point of view: Prague was the forty-third city in the world to have one. Thus, as a part of the official program, it was difficult to establish a myth of the construction's technical uniqueness. At most one could emphasize a few individual moments. The tunneling beneath the Vltava River between the Old Town Square and the Lesser Quarter, for example, was mythologized with the help of film (*The Song of the Tree and the Rose**) and the transferring of the tunneling shield without dismantling it was legendary in *People from the Metro*.[†] In this case, however, the technical values were actually subordinated to others. The contemporary journalistic profile of the tunneling indicated that news of the technology's success in the underground was competing with the insufficient possibilities for its patheticization: "The Soviet tunneling shield drilled from station to station like a mole."[21]

Moreover, in official conceptions of the metro, motifs emerge connected with its societal significance. The metro is not seen as a mere structure. Instead, it "far exceeds the framework of its original task, which was to satisfy the transportation needs of the inhabitants of and visitors to the city." This excess is expressed something along the lines of: "The metro's qualities raised our national pride with respect to a well-executed undertaking and the abilities of our Socialist generation. It had a significant effect on morally volitional qualities such as initiative, reliability, precision, and responsibility. It stimulated emotional feelings of beauty and aesthetics and contributed to the humanization of life. . . . It also proved the ability of Socialist society to resolve complex and demanding tasks, and it has become an instrument in the battle against despair, distrust, and indifference."[22] Furthermore, the metro (especially the architecture of its stations) is "the pride not only of the capital but of our entire Socialist society and of all who participated in this construction."[23]

These qualities are inscribed directly into the architecture where functionality often takes a backseat to conspicuous representation. In an unpublished manuscript, Bohuslav Blažek accurately describes the contradiction that distinguishes

---

* *Píseň o stromu a růži*, dir. Ladislav Rychman, Prague, 1978.
[†] *Lidé z metra*, dir. Jaromil Jireš, Prague, 1974.

the Prague metro.[24] It is a technological work, but it does not partake of the aloofness of technological civilization. It ostentatiously draws attention to its presence (the tearing down of a housing development to clear the view to the metro's entrance, the architectonic monumentalization of the ventilation system, and so on). According to the rationale of an underground structure, attracting attention to that which should remain hidden is "of course both functionally and semiotically ridiculous,"[25] but according to the rationale of the metro's official conception, which understood the work as an authoritative testimony to society, such externalization of the underground structure was of course entirely logical and proper.

This testimony reveals the entire strategy of the designation of the individual stations. Surprisingly few names referred simply to the aboveground locality in Prague (Smíchov Train Station, Můstek, Main Train Station, Muzeum, Kačerov, Strašnická, Radlická). On the contrary, we notice that often the localizing designation is deceptive and divorced from the topographical reality. For example, the Hradčanská Station is not near Hradčany at all, but rather in Špejchar. Malostranská is located outside of Malá Strana, more precisely in Klárov. The Vltavská Station is by Hlávkov Bridge, which is in its own way also by the Vltava River, but the river cuts through all of Prague, from north to south. Thus, the topographical designations identify nothing at all, especially because the street of the same name is in Smíchov. The station's name is usually a reference to a prestigious ideational value rather than a relevant topographical feature. Thus, the name of the metro station often completely loses its localizing function and does not refer to anything other than an ideological value.

One can distinguish several levels of ideological values, which are generally given preference. The first level is that of traditional national values, be they from the nation's past (Karlovo náměstí, Charles Square*), especially from the Hussite era (Želivského,† Jiřího z Poděbrad‡), or from the area of national emblematics in the widest sense of the word (Hradčanská, which refers to the symbol of Prague Castle, Vltavská, to the Vltava River, which holds an exceptional position in the national symbolisms, Národní třída [National Avenue], Náměstí Republiky [Republic Square]).

---

* Charles IV, King of Bohemia and Holy Roman Emperor from 1346 to 1378, is popularly referred to as *Otec vlasti*, Father of the Homeland.
† Jan Želivský (1380–1422) was a Hussite priest who was arrested and beheaded during the civil wars between the various Hussite factions.
‡ Jiří z Poděbrad (1420–71) was a Czech king and prominent Hussite.

Designations referring to the battle for national liberation during World War II were extremely frequent: Dukelská*, Sokolovská, Pražského povstání (Prague Uprising), Mayor Vacek,[†] Švermova,[‡] Fučíkova,[§] Czech workers and the Socialist movement are strongly emphasized (Gottwaldova,[**] Staroměstská—the pictorial representation in the station's entrance hall clearly suggested an implicit allusion to the events of February 1948[††]—Fučíkova, Švermova) and general Socialist emblematics (Mládežnická,[‡‡] Budovatelů (Workers), Družby (Friendship), Kosmonautů, Náměstí Míru (Peace Square). An unusually significant group of names were those referring to the ideological complex of friendship with the Soviet Union (Dukelská, Leninova, I. P. Pavlova,[§§] Sokolovská, Družby, Kosmonautů, Moskevská).

Of course, these ideological spheres were not in conflict with one another; in fact, the opposite was true: They became consolidated into a single comprehensive ideological value. Frequently, as we can see, a single name is incorporated into several of these artificially separated layers. In fact, it is precisely the indivisibleness of this comprehensive value that composes its fundamental quality: the national and Socialist tradition and friendship with the Union of Soviet Socialist Republics (USSR) are unequivocally presented as closely connected, even identical. They become a single signifier officially referring to the sign that is the metro.

Such a strong bias toward the semiotic side of the means of transportation, however, entered into conflict not only with traditional approaches to the semiosis of underground space, which strenuously tries to conceal, but which naturally also clashes with the practical functions of the underground railway. The

---

* Dukelská refers to Dukla Pass, near the town of Svidník in Slovakia along the Polish border. It was the scene of a battle in the fall of 1944 during the Slovak National Uprising.
† Václav Vacek was the first Communist mayor of Prague during the years 1945–54.
‡ Marie Švermová (1902–92) was a fanatical communist her entire life. In the late 1940s and early '50s she held high positions in the Community party and was a vigorous proponent of the '50s show trials.
§ Julius Fučík (1903–43) was a Czechoslovak journalist and active member of the Communist Party of Czechoslovakia. He was imprisoned, tortured, and executed by the Nazis and lionized by the postwar Czechoslovak Communist government.
** Klement Gottwald (1896–1953) was the first Communist president of Czechoslovakia.
†† The Communist putsch happened in February 1948.
‡‡ Mládežnická refers to a youth movement.
§§ Ivan Petrovich Pavlov (1849–1936) was a Russian physiologist, psychologist, and physician. He received the Nobel Prize in 1904 for research on the digestive system. Pavlov is best known for describing the phenomenon now known as conditioned reflexes with dogs.

ideological station names recalling "China of the Mao Zedong era"[26] often came
into conflict with the commonly used names (Gottwaldova and Gottwaldův
Bridge vs. Nuselský Bridge, Moscow vs. Anděl, Švermova vs. Motorlet,* Fučíkova vs. Holešovice Train Station) and remained puzzling from an orientational
perspective. Typical in this regard is the frequent and obvious onomastic arbi-
trariness: the terminal station of track III B, for example, bore the working title
of Únorové vítězství (February Victory), but finally received the name Dukelská.
From the perspective of the unified comprehensive signifier, it did not matter
which of the two were chosen (furthermore, let us not forget that the motif of
Victorious February had already been indirectly "occupied" by the Staroměstská
Station). We must note that it is precisely the disengaging from the practical
function that allowed the metro to operate as a sign signifying the ideological
complex "Czechoslovak Socialist Society."

It was still necessary for the Prague metro to incorporate the underground
railway more fully into the space of the city. This tendency of divorcing the metro
from the topography of Prague was finalized by the official emphasis on the
nationwide nature of the structure. This was reflected both in journalism, which
emphasized the role played by other regions in the metro's construction (the
Budějovická Station was built by workers from Budějovice; Kačerov by those
from Brno; Mládežnická by those from Plzeň; Pražského povstání by engineers
from Karlovy Vary, and so on[27]), as well as the general emphasis on the Czechoslovak character of the structure ("the construction of the metro is an example of
the mutual efforts of the Czechs and Slovaks, the linking of all regions of our
nation"[28]). Thus within Prague—or rather beneath it—an ideal world of "Socialist Czechoslovakia" was created through the medium of signs. From this stand-
point, the metro was presented as the completion of the cultural tradition of the
nation (of both nations): "Every historical era has bequeathed to Prague a marvelous legacy; under Socialism an immense, bold, and much needed work has
come into existence—the METRO."[29] It was characterized as an investment in
"the treasure house of historical national monuments,"[30] but at the same time, it
was primarily the manifestation of the success of the entire nation's efforts ("It
took innumerable / generations / from Great Grandfather Čech† / to get here /
to Gottwald's Bridge"[31]).

---

* Motorlet was a Czech engine manufacturing company nationalized in 1946. Among other
   engines, it produced the engine that powered the Soviet MiG-15.
† According to historical Legend, Czech tribes led by Grandfather Čech halted their journey
   at Říp, 50 kilometers north of Prague, and decided to settle there.

Architectonically, the metro belongs "somewhere between an exhibition hall and a mausoleum. Here you must take slow, shuffling steps, tilt your head back and to stifle the boredom, examine the ceiling, nudge yourself and whisper in wonder, lower your eyes with a melancholic expression; don't address anyone loudly, and should someone laugh, you should start in irritation."[32] This is how the sociologist Bohuslav Blažek describes the way the architecture accommodates the ideological function of the metro by emphasizing the dignity, seriousness, and splendor of the display.

Everything in this semantic sphere is ritualized. Real acts of cooperation between two countries are transformed into an external play of emblems (memorial plaques, the arrangement of the Moscow Station stop). Human labor is enveloped in a celebratory aureole of applause and homage; it is stylized by traditional methods laid down soon after the war under the influence of Soviet ideograms such as those of battle and struggle. The disagreement over the conception of the aboveground streetcar and the conception of the metro was seen as a battle between good and evil, and the structure itself as a battle against unfavorable geologic conditions (a similar mythicization of the underground took place in Moscow in the 1930s[33]), as a battle for the people's faith, and so on, and finally as the victory over the "crisis"* at the end of the 1960s and its fomenters. In his congratulatory poem on the occasion of the Supreme Leader's seventieth birthday, Miroslav Florian describes the grandiose image of the apotheosis of the president of the Czechoslovak Socialist Republic, Gustáv Husák, in which the participants included Prague, represented here by its river ("I would like to resound and flow like a waterfall"), Rye and Barley Streets ("they smell like salted bread crumbs, like malted barley!"), and also the metro:

Again and again, the metro brings rustling grapes
from Vinohrady. The earth is grateful
to the man who gave it his word, who took it to wife,
who maintained its bonfires during the Uprising
and managed to save it.[34]

It was perhaps Jiří Procházka's and Ladislav Rychman's film *Song of the Tree and the Rose* (1978) that most clearly created the official conception of the metro. All the elements of the idea are realized in the simple story of a Soviet

---

* The "crisis" refers to the Prague Spring.

engineer by the name of Kuznyetsov who arrives to assist with tunneling beneath
the Vltava River and who once again wages a battle in Prague just as he did thirty
years ago—in May 1945. The composition is built on the constant alternation of
scenes from May 1945 and "the present day"—the tunneling to Klárov. Nothing
is left to the viewer's conjecture: one of the protagonists, the Czech engineer
Franta, expresses the idea in full. For him, the tunneling is unequivocally "a battle for the city . . . for the people. . . . Do you understand?" And his interlocutor
engineer Kuznyetsov, indeed, understands: "Da, ya ponimayu!"* The noise of
pneumatic drills are compared to grenade explosions. At the same time—paradoxically, but in its own way true—there is no one to fight for because all the
people presented on screen are already "ours" in advance, whether they be musi-
cians ("with pleasure, the entire group submits to song," says the narrator) or the
public ("Wonderful. You are all wonderful!"). Even the youths in the club enjoy
themselves by singing the Russian song "Field, Little Field."

We must keep in mind when speaking of the semiotics of the Prague underground that two elements are engaged in battle. One element, the dark one, is
connected with disturbing images traditionally associated with the underground.
The other element, clear and optimistic, transforms the underground into a
monument of the Socialist era. The coexistence of these two elements is not of
course unproblematic. The semiotics of the Socialist ideal were set against the
chthonic forces of the underground and launched themselves into battle against
its demonic mythology with a mythology of its own. This mythology, to some
extent, penetrated the poetry of the period, which otherwise seemed to be engaged precisely in the archaic myth of the underground regarding the metro in
the 1970s and '80s. Of course this penetration did not lead to substantial artistic
results. The optimistic semiotics of the ideal introduced monumentality, emble-
maticness, and normativeness to poetry, returning it to shallow, post–February
1948 propaganda.

Moreover, it was difficult to naturally install the image of a "monument of
the Socialist era" in the underground. On the one hand, the attempt to entirely
semiotize the metro as signifying the abilities and traditions of Socialism necessarily transformed even certain negative architectonic and technical peculiarities
of the construction into an affirmation. Involuntarily and collaterally, the fact
that the metro creates entry barriers for the sick, mothers with children, and
invalids could also be semanticized. The voice ("screech of a crazed teacher"[35])

---

* Russian for "Yes, I understand."

driving children away from the broken white line along the platform acquires the grotesque image of a transparent allegory. On the other hand, one cannot overlook the fact that these other, dark semiotics of the underground threaten to demonize the sedulously constructed monument of the metro and transform it into "the other world," the realm of shadows.

If we compare the metro as an officially constructed and dispatched "text," as a "message" with, for example, the National Monument in Žižkov (and at the level of the general meaning of the message between both "texts" there is agreement), the Žižkov monument has the advantage of its position on a raised area ("above"), as well as the fact that it is set apart from the everyday life of the city. The celebratory emblematics of the metro, however, are plunged directly into the center of Prague's workaday world. To be sure, it sends out its message day after day to throngs of people, but at the same time this necessarily inures them to it. Travelers in the Prague metro walk beneath a panoramic portal in the south vestibule of the Moscow Station, the composition of which bears information celebrating Czechoslovak-Soviet friendship. On the platform, the paving made of red painted granite and the crimson marble of the trackage, in combination with the white vault, address the theme of "white stone and crimson Moscow," but the travelers are merely awaiting their train. Furthermore, the train was built in the Mytishchinsky factory,* which thereby repeated the message concerning friendship; travelers, however, have entered here to reach their entirely private destination. At the Gottwald Station, the existing white signs bearing the names of the station stops are suddenly replaced with meaningful red signs, "the reign of darkness is overthrown." Light falls into the wagons offering a view of Prague, but the passengers are simply traveling from their drab housing developments to work and back.

Of course, even the dark semiotics of the metro are subject to trivialization, but every metro system in the world is built so that it suppresses the effect of the powers of darkness. Every underground railway structure in effect says: You are certainly beneath the ground, but pay this no mind. Here, it is safe and calm; reliable, fast, and punctual transportation is here to serve you, which has only one goal—to transfer you wherever you like and then return you to the surface.

The dark meanings of the underground are accustomed to remaining covert; they do not try to dominate the overall significance. In short, the traveler passes

---

* Prague metro cars were built in the Mytishchinsky factory in the Soviet city of Mytishchi, 19 kilometers northeast of Moscow. The city is an important center of machine building.

through the turnstile, descends along the escalator into the depths, rushes through
corridors, dashes through dark tunnels in train cars, and never knows when he
will don the role of Orpheus wandering after his Eurydice, when he will recall the
ancient ritual of the obolus,* when, on the moving stairs, he will experience the
oppressive feeling of passing by and in the reflecting windows of the cars catch
sight of his own astonished face.

---

* The obolus (or obol) is a Greek silver coin. In ancient Greece, the deceased were buried
  with an obolus, placed beneath the tongue or on the eyes so that once a dead person's ghost
  reached the underworld of Hades, it would be able to pay Charon for passage across the
  River Styx.

11

Michurin

Ivan Vladimirovich Michurin (1855–1935) was a Russian horticulturist praised by the Soviet government for developing over three hundred new types of fruit trees and berries in an attempt to prove the inheritance of acquired characteristics. When Mendelian genetics—the transmission of hereditary characteristics from parent organisms to their offspring, named after the work of Gregor Johann Mendel (1822–84)—came under attack in the Soviet Union, Michurin's theories of hybridization, as elaborated by T. D. Lysenko, were adopted as the official science of genetics by the Soviet regime despite the nearly universal rejection of this doctrine by scientists throughout the world. The Michurin myth found fertile ground in Czechoslovakia. His ideas permeated agricultural practices and literary propaganda. The vision of transforming "imperfect" nature into an orchard not only asserted the unlimited possibilities of Socialist Man, but also completed the building of the joyous Socialist paradise.

The cult of the Russian horticulturist Ivan Vladimirovich Michurin spread from the Soviet Union throughout the newly established "people's democracies" and quickly took root. In Czechoslovakia, the cult helped construct the euphoric vision of the country as a blooming orchard ("in its orchards, my country is roseate in every respect"; "we are a flowering fragrant orchard"[1]). Even the celebration of Socialist large-scale industry willingly subjected itself to this characterization ("our factories, blooming orchards"; "effortlessly you will harvest coal like an orchardist"[2]).

The influence of Michurin's myth was so powerful in Czechoslovakia that even during Normalization in the 1980s, an attempt was made to revive it, at least in outline form. We see it in Jan Kozák's novel *Adam and Eve* (1982), the plot and hero of which preserve all the essential characteristics of the Michurin legend. The reference to the Russian orchardist is explicit, and the hero is in fact nicknamed Michurin. Moreover, the fact that the author himself claimed the story was based on the orchardist A. Koňas from Roudnice, a genuine orchardist, reinforces the hagiographic aspect, a necessary component of the Michurin myth. If we peel away the erotic facade, the focus of the story is the hero's efforts to set up a peach orchard "on a desolate hillside, overgrown with shrubbery and clumpy thistles," moreover on "the north side" somewhere in the Polabí Region. Because of his dream, the hero is "silenced and considered insane by all," but he himself accepts this as a challenge, as his life's destiny, as a possibility to "realize a miracle."[3] Kozák introduces the lucid and straightforward iconography of orcharding (trees, earth, grafting wax, bees, an apple) and emphasizes the conventional link to the biblical theme of Eden (even the romantic framework of the orchardist plot, even though foreign to the Michurin subject, contributes to the biblical theme, as does the choice of protagonists' names), as well as the sphere of national emblems in their classical Revivalist appearance. The author sets the story in a landscape characteristic of a Czech national myth—at the foot of the Říp Mountain, the mythical point of departure for the journey of Father Čech, the forefather of the Czechs.* Other orcharding emblems suggest national mythologization as well (bees and the linden tree are symbols of Czechness and Slavism as a whole). Of course, the entire forced national framework merely conceals the destruction of the generous frame of the Michurin legend, which in Kozák survives only in individual motifs. The novel as a whole sinks to the level of an intimate, personal story restricted to an individual fate and an isolated region.

At first glance, most of the details in Kozák's novel correspond, if only superficially, to that of the classical text that reinforced the Michurin myth after World War II, the Aleksandr Dovzhenko film *Life in Bloom* (1948).† In this film, we likewise find the Michurin theme of peach planting in the north, and his endeavors are also met with a lack of understanding. Finally, where Kozák employed the party secretary Pavel Sitar, Dovzhenko used representatives of the new revolutionary government and the historical figure of Kalinin.‡ Against this background,

---

* According to Czech legend, three brothers, Čech, Lech, and Rus, decided one day to seek out a new dwelling place and set out on a journey with their tribes. When they reached the Dnieper River, Rus decided that this was the place for his tribe to settle. Čech and Lech continued. Then Čech climbed to the top of Říp Hill in Bohemia and when he saw the vast fertile land, he decided to claim it for his people. Lech and his tribe continued their journey and settled in present-day Poland.

† *Life in Bloom* traces Michurin's life from its humble beginnings to his eventual development of over three hundred new plant varieties. The film's message is its suggestion that Michurin could never have achieved his cross-breeding miracles without the support of Bolshevik revolutionaries.

‡ Mikhail Ivanovich Kalinin (1875–1946) was a Bolshevik revolutionary and Soviet politician. He was the formal head of the Soviet State from 1919 to '46.

it is quite clear that Adam's adoption of Eva's son Tomek from her first marriage is actually a conventional Lysenko-Michurin* argument with the Mendel-
Morgans in which the qualities gained by cultivation are privileged over "mechan-
ical," "bourgeois" inheritance and the genetic dependence on parents, in other
words the "mentor" over "father": "It is true I did not conceive him, but he is
my son. He resembles me neither in body nor face. I do not recognize in him
my movements and gestures, but some of his characteristics and thoughts, yes.
Along with Eva, who gave birth to him, I breathed into him a soul—unfortu-
nately only later. I grafted it upon him, looked after it, and therefore he is Eva's
and mine."[4]

All this forms, however, only individual parallels. The essence of the Michurin
myth was its universality, and in the mid-1980s, this could no longer be revived.

The Michurin myth was intimately related to the universal Socialist emblem of paradise. Traditionally, paradise found its analogue in the "garden," the
"orchard,"[5] and the projection of the Socialist world as a representation of
paradise called for its concretization in the orchard metaphor. The semiotics of
Michurin's orchard asserted the unlimited possibilities of man, the imperfection
of raw nature, and the necessity of transforming it from its very foundations
according to human will. The Michurin vision of nature is certainly not a romantic illusion—on the contrary, it is imbued with dissatisfaction and a longing
for improvement ("It is nature . . . that is incorrect. Everything is growing somehow askew, growing incorrectly"[6]). Nature is perceived as an unrealized orchard
and therefore as a manifestation of human indifference and insufficient diligence
("Regrettable is this world. How I hate poverty and mental laziness. The alder,
aspen, pine, and willow—no matter where I look, nothing is as it should be,
nothing is human . . ."[7]).

From this perspective, authentic nature simply means the absence of an
orchard, a rejection of or even an offence against paradise. Simultaneously, it
is almost as if we can hear (and in the later Michurin hagiography it is actually
mentioned[8]) Turgenev's[†] declaration from his novel *Fathers and Sons*, "nature is
not a temple, but a workshop,"[9] which indicates that nature can be accepted only

---

* Trofim Denisovich Lysenko (1898–1976) was a Soviet biologist and agronomist who
rejected orthodox genetics in favor of "Michurinism," which became an assault on orthodox
genetics (called Weismanism-Morganism-Mendelism by Soviet propaganda). Michurin's
theory of the influence of the environment on heredity was a variant of Lamarckism.

† Ivan Sergeevich Turgenev (1818–83) was a Russian novelist. *Fathers and Sons* (1862) is
his most famous work and depicts a battle between the generations. The main character,
Bazarov, is a nihilist and often referred to as the first Bolshevik.

insofar as it lends itself to human exploitation, insofar as it becomes a "workshop" for the fulfillment of human intentions.

Thus in principle, the Michurin orchard is not sequestered off from the rest of the world. Its borders are not the physical borders of Michurin's experimental hybridization workstation in Kozlov. It is not separated from uncultivated nature like an oasis of cultivation and order. It opens outward. It is a fortress from which an attack is mounted against raw nature. The Michurin orchard aspires to spread throughout all of Russia, throughout the entirety of the Soviet Union, to seize the "neutral" landscape and transform it into an area artificially organized by man in harmony with his needs—into a "workshop." No matter how much the exclusivity of Michurin and his project is emphasized, the culmination of the Michurin myth is primarily the transformation of the Socialist world into an orchard by raising more and more "Michurins" ("every nation already has its own Michurin"), through the birth of millions of students of Michurin.[10] The aggression of Michurin's orchard, which seized nature and transformed it into gigantic projects by combining orchards and fields, by creating the so-called forest-orchards and so on, became analogous to the mammoth technical projects of the Soviets, such as the Kuybyshev and Tsimlyansk hydroelectric stations, the Volgadonsk canal, and so on, which just as radically encroached on the surrounding countryside. In both cases, nature was cast as the unambiguous antagonist, not at all as a partner—it was necessary to explicitly "defeat" her: "Grandpa Matvej's eyes shone: 'In the war we conquered Fascism, and now we shall conquer nature.'"[11]

The Michurin garden unambiguously offered the ideal, but at the same time, it presented the ideal as the only possible human reality. It embodied and concretized the paradisiacal image of socialism and especially the Soviet Union as a country that had achieved happiness, a country blossoming from the south all the way beyond the Arctic Circle ("the orchards are blooming beyond the Arctic Circle"[12]). At the same time, the Michurin myth presented this vision as the only genuine, authentic, and typical one. The contradiction between reality and this vision was seen as an anomaly. In this sense, the Michurin orchard could be—and actually was—an analogy for various social activities, all of which were directed toward the postulating of an ideal along with its simultaneous interpretation as the only genuine reality. Thus, the Russian author Alexander Fadeev could readily make reference to Michurin's orchard as a means to elucidate the fundamental ideological concept of the official art of the period, Socialist Realism: "The apple grown in a garden, especially in Michurin's garden, is an apple simultaneously both as it is and as it ought to be. This apple better expresses the essence of apples in general than do wild fruit. It is the same with Socialist Realism."[13]

The Michurin apple "as it ought to be" simply elucidated the true character of the Socialist world as such—in detail as well as in the whole. In this sense, the Michurin orchard was more of an ideological construct than a technical orchard project. In the specialized literature, the information about Michurin's own orchard technology also takes a back seat to ideological values. From this perspective Michurin's hybridization attempts lay the foundation for "progressive Soviet science," initiate the only correct "Michurin-Lysenko direction in biology," and do battle with "Mendelism-Morganism" (at the same time of course even "the question of affiliation to Mendelism-Morganism as a theory officially rejected in Czechoslovakia is simultaneously a political and ideological question signifying the direct rejection of a regime and therefore de facto betrayal").[14] Unscientific texts concentrated on the ideological value of the Michurin orchard even more. They emphasized the fact that the orchard's existence alone was a sign of the care the Bolshevik government devoted to the development of its land. According to these texts, the orchard bore "authentic" testimony to the genuine essence of Socialism, its ability to realize miracles. It also bore testimony to the personal qualities and wisdom of Vladimir Ilyich Lenin and Joseph Stalin, who appeared in the Michurin hagiography as protectors of the orchard.

One must emphasize that Michurin's orchard fits in precisely with the ideological context of the times because it stresses the theme of transforming nature ("Through the work in his garden, Michurin created an entirely new science—the science of transforming nature"). In the era of Socialism, orcharding became an appropriate allegory for the creative powers of the new man.[15] Incidentally, the transformation of nature was a favorite slogan even in Czechoslovakia, and in the 1950s it was a frequent theme in journalism and even literature ("We will force the land to give all that it can! . . . We will place that mountain range over there. . . . Tomorrow we will let fall some rain"; "Stand here, ye mountain! / And here, lower your brow!"[16]). This motif belonged to a much wider register of the complete and universal transformation of reality ("we will change life on earth"[17]), which applied both to its relationship to tradition as well as individual people, all of whom had been eyewitnesses to events of the recent past and therefore not adequately prepared for the new ethical demands that placed life in this new, fantasized epoch.

This general topos of "transformation" was realized in various metaphors. Frequently, it drew on the thematic sphere of plowing ("files of young men and women, / to plow up the past"; "tractors, tractors, / gloriously you shattered /

outmoded opinions, / the outmoded system!"[18]). Analogously, the topos of transformation frequently came from the thematic sphere of steel processing, whether it was smelting ("we even know how to make excellent steel / from the iron waste tossed aside"[19]), tempering, or forging ("with the hammer of battles we transform the person"; "he transformed people like a blacksmith transforms his red-hot steel"[20]).

From this perspective, cultivation and orcharding represented simply another thematic sphere to which the topos of transformation was linked. Every one of these spheres of course offered further limited possibilities through the emphasizing of other aspects of the topos. The metaphor of plowing emphasized the natural side of change (that which was impoverished had to be brought into a new state of fertility via transformation), and the metaphor of processing steel thrust into the foreground the motif of strength, even violence, which was necessary to realize the transformation. It was the thematic sphere of cultivation and orchard growing, however, that best suited the scope of utopia modeled according to the traditional Garden of Eden. It offered transformation, a value that simultaneously included the qualities of refinement, education, the discovery of the valuable in the seemingly invaluable, and the rejuvenation of the old. The imposition of the "desired" will on nature, on forms of life, on humans externally came to resemble kindhearted care, solicitousness, long-term patient interest: "When we change the desert into wheat fields, / we give the mountains a bright floral / dress from the fecund trees."[21]

In this way, Michurin himself achieved the same level as other "transformers" of reality who imposed their will and transformed it into what it should have been in principle—the only typical and authentic one. He stood alongside the leaders of the Bolshevik Revolution, and his biography, just like the biographies of other revolutionaries, leaders, and heroes, had to conform to the laws of the hagiographic genre, a sort of modern saint's life. In his biography, the motifs of Michurin's noble origin and his proprietary relationship to his experimental orchard were suppressed. On the other hand, other motifs were stressed: his loyalty to the revolution, his revulsion of tsarism, his love of Lenin and Stalin, his close relations with Kalinin (Kalinin actually paid a visit to Kozlov), his love of simple folk and his hatred of landowners, his nationalism and along with it his proud refusal of tempting offers by foreigners—"Americans" ("As always he refused foreigners. He did not sell them grafts from his magical roses, but he would allow his Russian people to take roses for propagation"[22]). Michurin penetrated the gradually developing Socialist pantheon along with a select crowd of leaders and revolutionaries. It is no coincidence that he was among those who lived to see idiosyncratic immortality in the Soviet Union—a geographic locality was given his name. This was standard procedure with geographic discoveries, and in this case it suggested that a brand new land was being discovered beneath the surface of old familiar Russia. In addition to Stalingrad, Leningrad, Kalinin-ingrad, Frunz, Ordzonikidz, and so on, the "new city" of Michurinsk was created by renaming Kozlov in 1932 (and thus during Michurin's lifetime).

Even Michurin was acquiring the attributes of a leader (as a teacher and a leader of millions of Michurins). He was labeled a revolutionary of science and nature, and in their turn, the leaders of the Socialist Revolution willingly assumed the relevant attributes of orchardist, a kindhearted caretaker of grafts. These elements became a standard component of the contemporary characterization of Stalin in the Soviet Union and Czechoslovakia ("You went to conquer / a garden for the shanties. Today it is already blooming, and my people as well are harvesting the fruit of your seedlings, / juicy fruit upon a laden platter"[23]), and in Czechoslovakia, of course, it became characteristic of Gottwald ("he, the orchard grower of better times"[24]).

There is one more significant reason the Michurin garden so easily became a model of the Socialist joyous era. According to the logic of the period and the laws of Socialism, the Socialist era appeared as the completion and conclusion of history. With the emergence of the joyous world of Socialism, any type of societal evolution had no meaning. Even though the orchard was a denial of pre-sumably chaotic and flawed nature, it offered only an ahistorical, natural scheme of time in a flawless, ideal version. Instead of "dialectical motion" toward new, still unknown and developing stages via a path of contradictions, it instead offered a regular and comforting pulsation of germination, growth, ripening, har-vesting, and new sowing.

12

Spartakiad

Spartakiad, first held in Moscow in 1928, was an international sporting event with which the Soviet Union attempted to oppose the Olympics. The word, however, was coined in 1921 by the Czech Jiří Chaloupecký and used to designate his own organization, which combined progressive revolutionary traditions with physical education. Until World War II, the word was used to designate workers' physical exercise celebrations in Czechoslovakia organized by the Communist party. The first rally was held in 1921 in a section of Prague called Maniny. During the Communist years, Spartakiad was a mass gymnastic display held every five years in Prague. It replaced Sokol, a nineteenth-century Czech patriotic gymnastic organization. Spartakiad linked physical education to the new state ideology and synchronized exercises into a single unified whole to demonstrate how human individuality gave way to the collective. The exercises portrayed the joyful life in Czechoslovakia, the loyal friendship with the Soviet Union, the love of peace, and the readiness to defend Socialism.

A campaign against the Sokol* movement was begun shortly after its eleventh meeting in 1948, when the organization demonstrated its disagreement with the Communist regime. At first, the campaign was directed against floor exercises, the very foundation of Sokol physical education.[1] In the beginning, the new conception of physical education favored purely athletic disciplines. Moreover, Sokol members could no longer count on the availability of Strahov Stadium, which had been built primarily for Sokol training. The possibilities of incorporating athletic disciplines into the overall plan of Socialist culture, however, were relatively limited; their prerequisite was individual performance, which could only vicariously become a sign of the abilities of the new society as a whole. The individuality of the performance itself concentrated too much attention on the individual, on his or her physical and volitional qualities. By contrast, the

---

* Sokol (Falcon) was a Czech gymnastic organization founded by Miroslav Tyrš and Jindřich Fügner in 1862. It was crucial in spreading the Czech national movement from the scholarly elite to the masses in the late nineteenth century.

rejected model of the Sokol rally contained elements that could clearly be utilized much more easily.

In 1954 officials reversed their decision and decided to make use of the tradition of the Sokol rally. Of course, this in no way signified the rehabilitation of the Sokol tradition. At the Third Nationwide Meeting of Propaganda Instructors, where preparations for Spartakiad had already been outlined, firm demands were made for the liquidation of the remnants of Sokol. Marie Zemanová, the chief spokesperson and director of the Propaganda and Agitation Section, complained: "I would like to draw attention to the fact that the old Sokol signs still have not been removed."[2] The organization outlined a strategy of how to confront and do battle with the past. Alexej Čepička's words in this respect are revealing: "Modern Socialist physical education and athletics cannot be brought into existence without doing battle against the old capitalist system of physical

"The 2nd Nationwide Spartakiad; Hurrah to the 15th Anniversary of Liberation; Prague, 23 June–3 July 1960." Artist: A. Zábranský. This poster was printed by the Department of Propaganda and Agitation of the Central Committee of the Communist Party of Czechoslovakia.

education and athletics." He points out the need to do away with remnants of the past: "The inauguration of Spartakiad must become a protest against bourgeois relics, as well."[3] At this time, much was expected from Spartakiad, primarily that it be victorious over "the existing state of the physical education movement."[4] At the same time, the role Sokol played as a predecessor to Spartakiad was never denied outright but rather shifted to the background, displaced by other large-scale physical education traditions—such as the Maninská Spartakiad and the so-called Workers' Olympics.* The participation of society as a whole in these events, however, was quite low.

This was not the first attempt to integrate the Sokol tradition into Socialist culture. Soon after February 1948, accommodating voices of the leading national representatives made themselves heard. Klement Gottwald announced that in several of its fundamentals, "the regime follows many of Tyrš's ideals, which express our best national traditions."[5] Václav Kopecký praised Sokol's "traditional character," "progressiveness," and "revolutionary spirit" with reference to the legacy of Garibaldi's red shirts.[6] It is characteristic that the first attack against the structure of Sokol was an attempt to transform it into a single athletic organization in which other athletic organizations would be dissolved. Sokol was not terminated, however, until 1952, and under its name physical education in villages was organized as one of the six components of a unified physical education program.

By 1954 Sokol rallies were remembered at most as merely a background, something with which Spartakiad had to be compared and which it had to overcome. At the same time, it is clear that this peculiar return to the rally's prototype was not a return to a concrete physical education value, but rather a return to a certain type of cultural code.[7] Sokol rallies thus represented a distinctive and highly ceremonial form of festivity (mass floor exercises before a large audience, parades through the city, performances by the army [beginning in 1920], athletic competitions, the veneration of the state, and links with other cultural events and ceremonies). From the outset, certain elements were tied to these forms—the demonstration of health, strength, self-defense, and Czechness. The last was hastily expanded after the formation of the Czechoslovak Socialist Republic—especially through the establishment of regional organizations in Slovakia and Carpathian Russia—as Czechoslovakness and Slavness, a thorn in the Germans' side. The possibility of exploiting these forms for a new message—that is, with

---

* The first Workers' Olympics took place in 1921 under the auspices of the Workers' Gymnastics Association (Dělnická Tělocvičná Jednota), an organization created to promote the physical, moral, and spiritual well-being of the working class.

their help to connect even physical education unequivocally to the new state ideology—appeared unusually tempting. At first sight, Sokol rallies could easily be adapted to the requirements of the period.

The more concretely the prototype of the Sokol rally was accepted as a model for Spartakiad, however, the more necessary it became to underscore the novelty and uniqueness of the enterprise. Naturally, this was sought in quantitative indicators, such as the unprecedented massive size of the exercises and the number of county and regional Spartakiads. From its inception, Spartakiad was also removed from the context in which it logically belonged: it was not seen as a simple physical education celebration, but as a paramount historical event. In 1954 the president of Czechoslovakia, Antonín Zápotocký, referred to Spartakiad in his New Years Address as a synecdoche of the entire country's efforts: "We look serenely into the future. We shall be neither nervous nor frightened. We shall continue our onerous labor to fulfill our plans, to develop our projects, and chiefly to prepare for the first nationwide Spartakiad."[8] Spartakiad was seen as a festivity explicitly linked to political celebrations. Characteristically, the days of Spartakiad were declared "glorious days" and thus as belonging to "the glorious days of May," to 1 and 9 May.* At the same time, Spartakiad was understood as a "paramount international political event."[9]

At first glance, the novelty of the Spartakiad undertaking seemed to inhere in a single element. Even though during the First Republic the Sokol movement and its functions were strongly statist—the rallies were certainly large and commanding—they were nevertheless the events of a physical education organization. Through its rallies, Sokol introduced itself to the public and paraded its presence and origins. The rallies were, to be sure, important events, but they were not universal—they were the rallies of the Sokols, nothing more. During tense historical moments (for example, at the end of the 1930s before the German invasion), the rallies could assume a distinctly symbolic function and suggest the attitude of the entire nation, but even then it was a pars pro toto: Sokol rallies represented the collective, it was its robust, morally upright component, fully able to defend itself. The type of festivity created within the bounds of the Sokol tradition certainly strove to create the illusion of national unity, but it was presented as a unity created by assuming the elite tradition of Sokol and its concepts of morality and life values. There was always something tautologically

---

* On 1 May, International Workers' Day was celebrated with a mandatory parade in all Communist countries, while 9 May marked the liberation of Czechoslovakia from Nazi occupation.

self-glorifying in the semantics of the rallies. The Sokol movement paid tribute to its own tradition and its own exclusiveness.

Unlike Sokol, Spartakiad did not recognize any such partial subject, even if it was meant to represent the entire collective. The participants of Spartakiad were not "gymnasts" gathering at Strahov Stadium and linked to one another by an exclusive, independent tradition that would elevate them above the rest. "Today . . . the masses will speak at Strahov stadium," declared President Zápotocký in his opening speech.[10] Indeed, the gymnasts at Strahov represented nothing less than "the masses," "the people." And even though numerous established Sokol motifs frequently repeated themselves at Spartakiad rallies, they assumed a different character. The popular slogan that "the stadium is not able to hold all those interested" no longer referred to the massiveness of Sokol and the passion of its members to participate in communal activities. It became rather a statement of the qualities of "the people" who realized the importance of Spartakiad and who were resolute in their decision to do everything possible to make it a reality. In the same way, the slogan proclaiming the "successful defiance of adverse weather" was a statement concerning not only the physical and moral maturity of the gymnasts but foremost the values of "the people."

If Sokol rallies were the "self-glorification" of Sokol, Spartakiad rallies were primarily the self-glorification of the people. Moreover, the individual performance elements developed within the tradition of the rallies were also seen as conforming to this semantic modification. The exercises of men and women, boys and girls of various ages and social groups, the performances of various organizational groupings (ROH,* SVAZARM†) and institutions (the army, the troops of the Ministry of the Interior)—these all served to present "the people" in all its diversity and yet as a "single" people, united in achieving a common goal.[11] In the same way, even the Spartakiad parades—which were also taken wholesale from Sokol, including the separation of the youth parade from the adult parade, which took place as early as the seventh Sokol rally in 1920—underwent this semantic modification. The original Sokol tribute to Prague, which hosted the rallies and demonstrations of "defiant Czechness," became something else. (Until the First Republic, the parades in Prague were led along the "German" aristocratic Příkopy Avenue, and the festivities held in Germanized Brno also assumed the character of a national demonstration.) Of course, the parades organized in the countryside represented the united people of Czechoslovakia

---

* ROH: Revoluční odborové hnutí (Revolutionary Trade Union Movement).
† SVAZARM: Svaz pro spolupráci s armádou (Union for Cooperation with the Army). This group prepared youth for membership in the Communist Party of Czechoslovakia.

with the peculiarities of the individual regions, but they were ceremoniously united by a mutual self-glorifying interest. The people marching through the streets of the capital paid homage to the Communist party representatives and the government and thus to the representatives of their own power, "the power of the people." Through them, they were paying tribute to their own sovereignty. Furthermore, the dance jamboree held at the Spartakiad Stadium, which was a component of the first Spartakiad rally, admittedly had its roots in the dances of the ethnographic performances of the Moravian Sokols during their fifth rally in 1907, but now it was given a different orientation. The dance troupes would gather here from all regions of the country to represent Czechoslovakia as a whole and demonstrate their mutual happiness as the unchangeable "condition of the soul" of the new Socialist people.

From the very beginning, Sokol counted on dramatic effect, and thus on the audience. Moreover, despite all attempts to make Sokol into an enormous organization, they counted primarily on non-Sokol members. The rally was a performance of Sokol's abilities and qualities for everyone else. Even though it remained a "theater," Spartakiad was merely the completion of the development toward a different rationale of performance—the connection of the gymnasts with the public in the galleries, the exercising representatives of the people with the onlooking representatives of the people. The participation in the stadium— either on the grounds or on the tribunes—was evidence of participation in a common undertaking, evidence of active participation in the cause of Socialism. The young poetess Jana Štroblová composed a poem about the atmosphere: "And it will happen, / that people on the tribunes / will suddenly hear / all hearts."[12] František Kožík developed the same theme in a 1955 article that proclaimed: "Our hearts beat simultaneously with the hearts of the gymnasts." Spartakiad was perceived as "the next great step forward—toward a reduction in the number of witnesses to the cause of Socialism and an increase in the number of its builders."[13] "The most glorious thing these days of Spartakiad provide us with is precisely that simple and massive 'we,' whose strength we perceive with our entire being," states Jan Kopecký in his 1955 article "A Glance into the Audience."[14] Of course, all these are merely verbal constructions, but the aim of their semantic intent is obvious: Spartakiad was supposed to be a project that would obliterate the border between audience and performers, a project during which the "gymnasts" and the "onlookers" become mutual participants in the selfsame ritual, in the communal creation of the image of life in a Socialist country. For that reason, Spartakiad necessarily became the cause of every citizen, whether he or she took part in the exercises or in the obligatory campaigns in its honor, whether he or she participated as a gymnast or spectator of regional, district, or nationwide Spartakiads, or made sacrifices through gifts and financial contributions.

Spartakiad became a "universal art," and even in this respect took over and brought to completion the original impetus of the Sokol rallies. Spartakiad offered the collective creation of a single aesthetic-ideological utterance as opposed to the individuality and privacy of artistic creation, which was at the time called into question and rejected but nevertheless difficult to suppress. It combined physical exercise, dance, music, the plastic arts, literature (poetry was often recited at the rallies), and theater. It was as if earlier dreams of *Gesamtkunstwerk* or avant-garde notions of the decline of art and its dissolution in a new collective super-genre were resurrected—dreams of poetry that would "leap off the paper, out of books so that life itself would become poetry!"[15]

Art found itself in the sphere of Spartakiad and its rituals, of course even vicariously, by becoming the fabric of art, film, music, literature, and especially poetry. Poetry in particular became Spartakiad's fundamental metalanguage: It presented the interpretation of the compositions, translated its nonverbal signs into straightforward verbal form. It was an obvious attempt to stabilize the meaning of the individual compositions and activities of Spartakiad much more firmly than their scripts called for, which frequently provided only a rough outline of the ideological value and were marked too much by interest in the physical education component of the performance. Spartakiad and the community spirit, along with the synthetic nature of its form, represented a clear challenge to intellectualism and literary pretentiousness, to "lofty and wispy words" (Pavel Kohout asserts, "Here ends invention, the play of lofty and wispy words that are born and die like mayflies. In their place, other words catch fire in our hearts, those of an unchanging value"[16]). Poetry associated with Spartakiad actually became part of the ritual, a component of its semantic utterance, as if through this association it was ridding itself of the danger of hollow verbalism and could arrive at elemental, "nonliterary" values.

In this connection, the semantic weight of all compositional elements and other Spartakiad functions grows remarkably. By comparison, the former Sokol exercises seemed no more than a purely formal construction, empty of content. Spartakiad, on the other hand, semanticized and ideologized everything: "Motion no longer exists merely for motion's sake. Every performance has its own meaning, its own idea, comprehensible and effective," notes Jiřina Dumasová.[17]

In the most general sense, the semantics of Spartakiad emerged from very basic elements. Such an enormous physical education campaign presented first and foremost the theme of the individual dissolving into the crowd. Before the war, even Marxist journalists at Sokol rallies were sensitive to such expressions of massiveness and collectivization and commented on them ironically: "Once again Prague will become a stage of massive nationalistic manifestations," wrote Ladislav Štoll in the 1930s. "The parade of thousands of hale, militarily disciplined gymnasts will send the on-looking crowds into rapture. The illusion of a fleeting image of a mechanically flawless performance, of the activity of healthy muscles, of stirring rhythms in the music of marching bodies amidst fluttering colored paper will stick in the minds of the audience and will once again temporarily draw a veil over the reality of society's anarchy and class struggle."[18] Such criticisms of Spartakiad no longer applied. Spartakiad became a conscious expression of a new way of life in which human individuality gave way to the collective; solitude was an unhealthy escape from the community, even a betrayal, a provocative unwillingness to participate in a common task. It was precisely the theme of an individual's dissolution into the whole, into the enormous kettle of Spartakiad that blossomed in contemporary poetry and journalism ("sixteen thousand boys and girls . . . are one being"[19]). Jarmila Urbánková, for example, in a poem responding to a club dance by the women of ROH, described an image of "a blue tide" flooding "the Strahov field." She added: "It is in vain to search for / the one, the one that is yours— / she has drowned in a sea of women, / she has dissolved in song."[20] A theme that might at first evoke a sense of apprehension—"the loss of a loved one," her "drowning," "disintegration"—is presented from an entirely different perspective. The loss of identity and uniqueness was redeemed by the discovery of a new horizon of a higher value.

The multitude into which individuals homogeneously dissolved was, however, also an unmistakable referendum, a "public voting act in which our country, our regime will be gloriously victorious."[21] It was proof "that . . . the people stand unwaveringly behind the Communist Party of Czechoslovakia and their government, that the people joyfully witness their intrepid and well-developed plans brought to fruition."[22] The enormous number of people submitting to the firm discipline of a conscientiously and scrupulously planned sports spectacle paradoxically became a sign of the spontaneity of the entire enterprise, as if to convey that such an enormous number of gymnasts submitting to a single production could not have been brought by force to Strahov Stadium and other stadiums throughout the republic. Thus, it must have been proof of a voluntary decision. The formidable ideological charge of Spartakiad extended this "voluntary decision" of support to the new regime as a whole, along with its foremost representatives. The navigation bridge from which the exercises in the stadium were organized had its symbolic double in the main tribune, where the representatives of the party and government assumed their seats. In the same way, just as the gymnasts represented the Czechoslovak people, the tribune represented "the party and the government." The actual performance, then, was the communication between the people and "the party and the government," during which the people affirmed their support of and devotion to the agenda of Socialism, and their gratitude for proper leadership ("today you see how beautiful a person can be when he is cared for"[23]). "The party and the government" accepted this confirmation and demonstrated complete identification with the people by their presence at the stadium. This all-embracing declaration of unity and the identification of everybody with everyone else—Czechs with Slovaks, men with women, children with adults, workers with the intelligentsia, and the people with the party—was tantamount to a declaration of the unity of "the people" and the constituents of the regime's power.

Another factor played a substantial role in the semantics of Spartakiad—the suppression of the incidental in favor of order, an essential part of Spartakiad activities. It was important that order and organization not be seen as an external principle, as something for which it was necessary to sacrifice the naturalness of human behavior, but rather as the inner essence of the human being, which was deformed in everyday life, and which was only perceived here at Spartakiad. "Cleansing" movements "of unsightly involuntary habits" were discussed in this respect.[24] Nothing was seen as divorced from life in the stylization of Spartakiad exercises. It was rather the ideal, which should be realized even in everyday life: the removal of individual spontaneity and arbitrary motion in favor of a single action organized from a single center. A yearning was created for such an anchoring of "Spartakiad motion" in everyday life ("after all, everyone should know how to march and line up straight, keep in step and stay aligned while marching"[25]). Reproaches were even made against the less-organized May Day parade, that it did not achieve the perfection and coordination of individual human gestures that Spartakiad did.

The unifying factor of the mass performances generated conditions for unification even at the level of such values as "beauty," "tenderness," "happiness," and on the other hand "work," "strength," "struggle," and "defense." Spartakiad bore testimony to the fact that in the world of Socialism, "happiness" is a universal feeling—in fact the only feeling—that "beauty" is a universal aesthetic category, and that even "work" is only an aspect of this all-embracing "happiness" and "beauty." The emblems of work were at the same time emblems of beauty—for example, in the exercises of the workers' reserves, the groupings of female and male gymnasts created cogwheels that gradually assumed the image of flowers ("the land of advanced industry, which is in the hands of its people, must bloom, after all!" noted a contemporary journalist[26]). Even the women's exercises, which more than others could emphasize values of an aesthetic and emotional nature, were identified with the motif of labor. Traditional sporting equipment assumed other values as well. The club became a symbol of a work implement, a spinning wheel a sickle or other such tool. The former Sokol sporting accouterment, the iron pole in the boys' performance, became a symbol of a farm tool. In the women's exercises, stylized work in the village was emphasized.

Women's performances, moreover, contained elements of military exercises, which heretofore had been primarily the domain of the men's performances. The motifs of work (for example, exercises with cubes symbolizing the building of Communism) and explicitly military elements appeared profusely, even in the exercises of children and adolescents. The exercises of soldiers with children, which were consistently oriented toward the theme of "the Czechoslovak army—the army of peace," culminated with the blast of a bugle, which interrupted an informal children's game, whereon the children left the area of the stadium together with the soldiers, thus demonstrating even their readiness to defend the motherland. The exercises of the sixth to eighth graders included grenade throwing, crawling, carrying wounded, and so on. The Spartakiad performances were stylized as "a mosaic of dazzling beauty," but at the same time it was emphasized that "its colors are not defenseless."[27] It was "gentleness—but also a fist," as Miroslav Florian described in his poem.[28]

The exercises, however, did not function only by a simple syntactic construction—with a paratactic placing of individual emblems next to one another and connecting them via analogies—some fundamental plots linking testimonies to the past with testimonies to the present and future were built within the compositional frameworks. In particular, the exercises of the men of ROH were constructed around one such linear story of a long journey that the working class had to undertake before it could achieve a joyous life in Socialism. The libretto of a DSO* exercise suggested a similar tale portraying the development of a Czechoslovak village from capitalism to the present. An exercise by the army depicted the difficult time during the World War II occupation, the resistance, and final joy of victory.

In other parts of the program, similar sentiments were expressed with metaphor, for example in the exercises of the youngest where the central theme of the

---

* DSO: Dobrovolná sportovní organizace (Voluntary Sports Club).

golden gate appeared as a symbol of society's crossing from "the old world" into the "new world" of Socialism ("children, follow me through the golden gate / onward to peace, onward to happiness, / onward to the gold that lies before us"). (By the way, this was in complete contradiction to the function of this motif in folklore: "The Golden gate is opened; those who enter are beheaded.") Spartakiad marches were also utilized as a way to shape the theme of "the road" as an image of the country's denizens traveling toward Communism. Thus, it was common to hear cheers and slogans during the march that were not directly related to Spartakiad ("The greater the number of farming cooperatives, the better off will we be!"). The slogans were bound together by the symbolic meaning of the march, which was obvious even to a foreign observer. For example, the Swedish author Arne Hirdman wrote that the celebratory marches "were not mere marches or exhibitions, but rather a march of the youth into life, a march of Czechoslovakia into the future."[29] Either way, the confrontation of the present with the past was almost always the subtext of any Spartakiad act: Spartakiad was a stylized testimony to the joyful Socialist present and future, and thus, by comparison, also a testimony to the suffering of the workers in the West, just as it was a testimony to the difficult life of the past. That is why the exercises of the children and youth occupied such an important position in the overall composition of Spartakiad. Children and youth were a traditional and, in the overall emblematics of Socialism, frequently used and abused symbol of the new era. Youth was depicted as a generation of Communism not burdened by the heritage of the past, a model generation perfectly embodying the new ideals.

A distinct semantic orientation was given to Spartakiad by its link with the anniversary of the Soviet Army's liberation of Czechoslovakia. The first Spartakiad was held on the tenth anniversary of the liberation. The decision to repeat Spartakiad every five years made it a component of the celebrations of the republic's liberation and therefore also a component of celebrations of friendship with the Soviet Union thereafter. This provided a solid orientation to the already clearly ideologically loaded mass expression of joy that accompanied Spartakiad. On the one hand, "happiness" was a general expression of the people's satisfaction with life under Socialism, but at the same time, it was a rendering of thanks to the Soviet Union for liberation and for pointing out the proper "historical path."

These fundamental semiotic mechanisms were then completed and perfected through numerous secondary methods. Color symbolism played a central role during the individual performances: white, blue, and red symbolized Czechoslovakia; red by itself symbolized revolution; blue was the color of peace but also the color of the proletariat, the color of coveralls; white was the color of peace;

yellow symbolized the sun and fields of grain, happiness, abundance, a rich harvest, and so on. The multidimensional discourse of Spartakiad was completed by the discourse of flags and banners (the national flags of the Czechoslovak Socialist Republic and the Soviet Union, tricolors, red ribbons, the flags of the people's democracies, a blue flag with a white dove as a symbol of the world "peace movement"), groupings of gymnasts into multicolored figures (circles as a sign of unity, a red star as a sign of Communism), into simple words and abbreviations (KSČ [Communist Party of Czechoslovakia], SSSR [USSR]), the overall arrangement of slogans on placards as well as chanted slogans, and so on.

In its entirety, Spartakiad was an attestation no different from those created by other contemporary semiotic constructs. Incidentally, the entire period of the 1950s was oriented toward maximal semantic reduction to a specific limited register of themes and methods of arrangement. Spartakiad was exceptional in its monumentality. It became an enterprise in which the inhabitants of the country metamorphosed into signs. Within the framework of Spartakiad festivities they cast away their uniqueness and nonsubstitutability and were transformed into mutually exchangeable stones in the overall mosaic. By assuming the position assigned to them, they reported the news given to them in advance concerning the joyful life in Czechoslovakia, the loyal friendship with the Soviet Union, the love of peace and the readiness to defend the achievements of Socialism, the readiness to fulfill "the bold plans" of the leading representatives, and so on. The laws of the mosaic—which engulfed all into one and dissolved the difference between the leading representatives and the people, between the actors and the spectators—did not allow one to ask what this "illusion of a fleeting image of a mechanically perfect collective act" was concealing. Not even Tristan Tzara,* the creator of Dada, who was among the spectators of Spartakiad, had the slightest suspicion when he proclaimed in an interview: "I feel I am in the very center of a free and joyful people who are conscious of their marvelous prospects."[30]

---

* Tristan Tzara (1896–1963) was a Romanian poet and essayist who founded the artistic movement Dadaism.

13

Renaming

One of the first things to be transformed during any societal change is the names of streets and squares. In Czechoslovakia, renaming became all too common due to the political and historical upheavals of the twentieth century. Surprisingly, the new names reflected not only the latest ideological reality but also the inherent need for continuation and custom.

A regime change always signifies an intervention into "the semiotic world" of a given community and thereby a metamorphosis of the corresponding sign system, an immense exchange of signs. The more closely a sign is linked to a certain valuational reference directly connected to official ideological conceptions—whether it be a monument, statue, pseudonym of a writer, name of an institution, or form of address—the greater the possibility that it be removed or substituted. Sometimes it is sufficient that the sign be at least only theoretically linked to the ideological conceptions. Even an ideologically innocuous sign can fall victim if it is perceived by the new regime as so valuationally inert that it would be advantageous to exchange it for an ideologically positive sign. Not even the names of cities, villages, mountains, or even personal names are exempt—recall, for example, the mass Slavicization of German surnames in Czechoslovakia immediately after World War II, especially in Eastern Europe, where until recently ideologues delighted even in usurping geographical reality (even at the cost of annulling old or ancient names representing an important—but, from a myopic propagandistic perspective, uninteresting—cultural value).

Traditionally, however, the first things to be transformed during any societal change are the names of streets and squares. In these cases, convention—as well as, apparently, the necessity of a large number of mutually noninterchangeable names—presupposes drawing on appellations designating not only some immediate realia or quality objectively connected to the location in question, but, on the contrary, to a certain "free," topographically nonbinding cultural value. Sometimes this cultural value is represented by the name of a person, momentous

event, historically valued emblem, and so on. During a regime change, this onomastic zone easily enters into an ideological competition with the new order and
becomes "an ideological relic" of the past calling for its own removal, which would
once again establish a fragile harmony between the name and the societal norm.

The history of naming streets and squares becomes a paradoxical seismo-
graph of historical reversals. Sometimes the appellative impulse fluctuates between
two extreme values: from the very beginning, for example, one and the same
street in Brno has been alternately referred to as either Bismarck Street or Peace
Street, according to how acceptable the connotations were, on the one hand,
of "Germanness," "German aggression," and "German military victory," and, on
the other hand, "war" and "peace."

Other times, the onomastic history of a municipal location is less clear. In
1925 Pod Kinskou (Below Kinsky* Square) in Prague was renamed Štefánik
Square.[†] During the Protectorate, it became Albrecht Square after nearby Albrecht
Barracks.[‡] In 1951 the name of the square was changed to the Soviet Tank Crew,
and today the name has become something more closely resembling the original: Kinsky Family Square.

The annulled name is not always wiped out entirely, however; frequently
it survives as an unofficial component of the official name, waiting to be recalled
and again made official years later. Sometimes it seems as if at least a part of the
original name adheres to the location, perhaps merely as a connotative nuance
or a scarcely perceptible semantic intention, which persists even in symbiosis
with the new name and often appears to influence the choice of name in advance.
The street On the Marne, named after the victorious battle of the French-British
military, which had prevented the German occupation of France, was renamed
Memel Street during the Protectorate to commemorate the military annexation
of Klaiped-Memel by Germany in 1939. In 1952, as a reaction to the Korean
War, the street was renamed Korea Street. Thus, the same "military" motif is
apparent throughout.

We see this in the changes after November 1989 as well. The street that once
bore the name of Ljuba Ševcová, a member of the Young Guard and the Komsomol, was renamed Svojsíkova Street after the founder of the Czechoslovak

---

* The Kinskýs are one of the oldest Bohemian families.
† Milan Rastislav Štefánik (1880–1919) was a Slovak politician, diplomat, astronomer, and
  Czechoslovakia's war minister during World War I. His actions contributed significantly to
  the cause of Czechoslovak sovereignty.
‡ Albrecht von Wallenstein (1583–1634) was a Habsburg military commander and one of the
  major figures of the Thirty Years' War.

Scouting Organization Antonín Svojsík (1876–1938). Thus, we see that some sort of common attribute of "youth" remained when the name was changed to designate scouting rather than the Komsomol.

At other times, it was the audio or graphic similarity that survived, at least partially, and the creators of this cosmetic adjustment, the guarantors of the new ideational accord between the name and the order, were satisfied with a mere adjustment in meaning. The street dedicated to Nadezhda Krupskaya* in Teplice was inconspicuously changed to Krupská Street, as if it had always referred to the nearby village of Krupka. In Prague, 7th of November† Street suddenly became November Street. This version is acceptable even today. In Mikulov, General Svoboda‡ Street became Svoboda, or Freedom, Street. Grotesque compromises were often reached between custom and the need for change.

Incidentally, even the swift and radical exchange of one ideological name for another (for example the transformation of Five Year Plan Street to Czechoslovak Exile Street) actually preserves an impression of its predecessor precisely in its lofty, although up-to-date, ideational content.

Cities and villages renounced names that conveyed information referring to Socialism, but even during this new phase of onomastic transformation, ideology was not done away with altogether. Just as all villages used to have their obligatory Lenin Street, today "progressiveness" is demonstrated with T. G. Masaryk streets throughout the country. Homage to contemporary heroes replaced homage to old ones; old ideograms were exchanged for contemporary ones. However, even though old signs are frenetically replaced with new, the old structures inevitably shine through.

---

* Nadezhda Krupskaya (1869–1939) was a Bolshevik revolutionary and wife of Vladimir Ilyich Lenin.
† The Russian October Revolution took place on 7 November 1917.
‡ Ludvík Svoboda (1895–1979) was a Czechoslovak military leader and politician. He was president of Czechoslovakia during the Prague Spring and ordered the Czechoslovak Army not to resist the invasion of Warsaw Pact troops.

14

Minus-Stalin

The city of Prague once boasted the largest monument to Stalin in the world. The 30-meter statue stood atop Letná Plane overlooking the city's historical center. It was erected in 1955 and built to endure an eternity. Seven years later, however, the massive structure was demolished to keep in step with Moscow's already dismantled cult of personality. In 1991 a 25-meter metronome, recalling the city's musical past, was placed on Stalin's plinth. However, because this is only a temporary sculpture, an intense discussion has begun among sculptors and historians about what ought to stand in Stalin's place.

The literary critic and semiotician Yuri M. Lotman coined the term *minus-priem* or "minus-device" to describe a phenomenon in the world of human creations and ideas in which absence is not always absence. A missing acoustic correspondence at the end of two prose sentences is something quite different from the sudden absence of a rhyme in a line from a regular hexastich, for the missing rhyme still carries with it the expected rhyme.[1] Something similar, but on a larger scale, is happening on Letná Plane in Prague. The empty space left gaping after the removal of the Stalin monument is not and will not in the near future be a genuine empty space. Whatever will be placed on this ostensibly vacant site will immediately enter into a semiotic relationship with the monument that had briefly stood there before, which is precisely what happened with ordinary potatoes that were stored in the entrails of Letná Plane in the 1960s. Whatever is constructed here will not merely stand as a structure but rather as a "structure on the site of the Stalin monument." It will absorb meaning from the statue that stood here before.

Of course, the meanings of the original arrangement will not penetrate the new structure in too much detail. The former monument by Otakar Švec thoroughly fulfilled the myth of the time concerning the identification of the people with their leader. The relief figures to the side symbolized the people and flowed into the immobile monumental figure of the generalissimo. He wore a simple

military overcoat; his left hand held a book (a sign of wisdom), and his right hand
was tucked in his bosom. Prague humorists saw in this movement an explicit gesture: he was reaching for his wallet.* This, however, was merely a carnivalesque
reduction of an obvious Napoleonic pose, which (along with the military overcoat) stated: here stands the commander.

The people were portrayed in two different images, which was also very
telling. On the eastern side, four figures symbolized the people of the Soviet
Union. At the head, a worker hoisted high a fluttering flag, a sign of victory, the
typical attribute of a representative of the victorious class and its battle path. The
figure of the scientist, clearly the successor of Michurin's† legacy, represented
the new intelligentsia of Socialism, which did not shut itself off from society in
dusky reading rooms and offices, but worked side by side in the field with the
others. The female partisan evoked victory in the war, which itself represented
the victory of the people. The western side of the monument displayed an allegory of the Czechoslovak people. Here too stood a worker at the head clutching
a flag. Behind him, a female cooperative farm member (with a sickle and an ear
of grain) turned slightly toward a man who doubtlessly represented a member of
the working intelligentsia (an almost loving gesture, but also a symbol of the
unity between intellectuals and the people). At the end of each line stood facing
the rear a Soviet and a Czechoslovak soldier wielding guns.

This backward glance, of course, bore enormous semantic weight. Although
the soldiers were actually facing northward, toward Bubeneč,‡ the gaze was meant
to face unequivocally to the west, that is, to the West. It was oriented in the opposite direction of the gaze "forward," which (with the single exception of the
Soviet scientist Michurin, who was obviously holding out his cheek toward the
sunrise) characterized the remaining figures. Not even the female cooperative
farm member and the intellectual, who were somewhat facing one another in the
"Czechoslovak" relief, were looking at one another. They too were gazing in the
specified direction, that is, in the direction of Stalin's gaze. If a gaze forward
unmistakably meant looking toward the future, then a gaze backward necessarily
meant looking toward the old world, one that was admittedly without a future

* The people of Prague dubbed the formation the "lineup for meat." Indeed, lineups were a
  daily occurrence throughout the entire country due to severe shortages of food and other
  goods. Thus, Stalin's Napoleonic gesture, in this reading, signified nothing more than reaching for a wallet within his coat. His happy demeanor was understandable; he was the first in
  line and thus guaranteed a piece of meat, a commodity in high demand.
† See chapter 11 on Michurin in this book.
‡ Bubeneč is a quiet residential area near the Prague Castle. Many embassies are situated
  there.

Monument to Stalin, 1955 (photo by Josef Klimes)

but was still a threat. It testified to the vigilance of the people and their readiness to defend.

The parallel positioning of figures in the Czechoslovak and Soviet sections of the statue, their interconnectedness in a single granite mass and assembly behind a common leader, testified to the indissoluble unity of the Soviet Union and Czechoslovakia. At the same time, the different conceptions repeated the nineteenth-century Revivalist model: the Czechoslovak "people" were perceived more lyrically, the Soviet more monumentally (contemporary evaluations of the project likewise commented on this aspect of the sculpture). Already in the early nineteenth century, the Czech poet F. L. Čelakovský* commented on this opposition. In the commentary to his verse collection *Echoes of Czech Songs* (1839), he discusses the antithesis of the Russian (heroic) and the Czech (lyric) national soul. Now, however, this opposition was enriched with new meanings: the monumental stylization of the Soviet people emphasized their role as a model and stressed their more immediate proximity to the ideal, as well as their more fundamental bond with the leader.

The attribute of monumentality naturally belongs primarily to him, but of course the leader merges with the people (both Czechoslovak and Soviet, with people in general) into a single stone mass heralding a statesman who both emerged from and personified the people, as well as celebrating the people who achieved fame and power through their statesman. At the same time, however, the statesman remained unique. His size, his placement at the head of the procession, and his motionless composure stood in contrast to the "petrified gestures" of the other figures, for example the raising of the fluttering flag and the vigilant turning of the head. Against the petrified temporality of the people, Stalin stood entirely in timelessness, outside of time, like Eternity itself, like the personification of Father Time.

Only an outline remains of that former meaning-laden construction on Letná Plane. But it appears that precisely the theme of time, which was to be denied in the name of the illusory and venerated eternity, hovers somewhere here in the air above the square blocks of the plinth. It is toward this desolation that the roads of the Letná Gardens converge and the stairs from the embankment theatrically ascend.

For this reason, it seems, Vratislav K. Novák decided to erect a statue of a metronome in this space.[2] The 25-meter pendulum entered into a dispute with

---

* František Ladislav Čelakovský (1799–1852) was a Czech folklorist and poet. Beginning in 1822 he collected Slavic folk songs, which he later imitated in his own books of verse, *Echoes of Russian Song* (1829) and *Echoes of Czech Song* (1839).

Demolition of the Stalin monument, 1962 (photo by Josef Klimes)

The Metronome (photo by Michael Batuzich)

the absent yet nonetheless present Stalin, which during the occasion of the jubilee exhibition began to measure out time to proclaim the end of eternity and the fall of the monument.

No matter how the space is resolved architecturally, the dispute with Stalin will be its destiny one way or another. Incidentally, even if the project of Madak Schneider had succeeded, which tried to replace the metronome with a purely aesthetic play of water, it would not have created merely "beauty without purpose" on this enchanted spot. It would have immediately become a political statement. In its own language, it would profess time and eternity, movement and monumentality. To paraphrase the verses of Omar Khayyám,* it would proclaim that old water is better than new empires.

---

* Omar Khayyám (1048–1131) was a Persian mathematician, poet, and astronomer. During his lifetime, he was renowned in his country for his scientific studies, but he is known to the Anglophone world as the author of the book of poems *The Rubáiyát of Omar Khayyám.*

15

The Celts within Us

The original inhabitants of Bohemia were the Celts, who appeared in the region about five hundred years before Christ, and it is from the name of one of their tribes, the Boii, that Bohemia got its name. Czechs often contend that they are descended from the Celts, but this is pure Romantic fantasy. The National Revivalists claimed to find elements of their Celtic heritage everywhere, and after November 1989, the Czech "cult of the Celts" seems to have been picked up again.

When we open the new *Great Czech Cookbook*, published in 1992 shortly before Christmas, we read in the introduction, somewhat taken aback: "In the beginning, our lands were the original homeland of the Celts, who gave it not only its name but also their ability to borrow creatively all that is remarkable and exceptional from other nations. The Celtic substratum became combined with our country's Slavic roots. Of course, cooking was done differently in the court of Charles IV and in the settlement around the castle, but one thing was the same. Czech cooks were always present with their skill and diligence. Of course these qualities bring us suspiciously close to countries in which the descendants of Celtic tribes who originated in Bohemia live today. Along with mistletoe, fairy tales, Blaník knights,* military vehicles and battle songs thundering from Hussite choirs, as well as the Celtic search for the proper faith, we transferred to the present day not only stories and myths, but also the Celts' creativity, acceptance of the good and aversion to violence, faithfulness to ideals, skillfulness and diligence."[1]

That nation, whose power in Europe was concentrated at one time on our territory and which provided the country we inhabit with a name (Bojohemum, Bohémie), stimulates our imagination. We find incontrovertible and enchanting traces of their distant presence in the towns of Stradonice u Berouna and Závist

---

* Legend has it that the Blaník knights will emerge from Blaník Mountain to save the country from its invading enemies.

u Zbraslavi.* Without a doubt, we were not in this region from the beginning. They were here earlier.

It thus comes as no surprise that at the dawn of our modern history, what we lacked in our own past we sought to discover with the help (actually at the expense) of that mysterious people who resided here from the fourth to the first century BC. Analogously, we tried to expand Czech history by associating it with larger Slavic events, which included a much vaster geographic area and a greater number of people. But because this was insufficient to attract the gaze of "educated Europe," we tried to "discover" a linkage between Czech (and Slovak) history and the prestigious history of antiquity. In the nineteenth century a number of Revivalist dreamers attempted to place the Slavs (and thus the Czechs) among the ancient Greeks or the Romans. See, for example, the work of Řehoř Dankovský and František Šír.†

The renowned poet Ján Kollár‡ dedicated his extensive work *Staroitalia Slavjanská* (Old Slavic Italy) to these efforts. During a trip to Italy, he himself experienced the enthusiasm of discovering Slavic life beneath the veneer of everyday Italian life: "In the past I had invented for myself Lord knows what notions about the much trumpeted polenta; but the moment I beheld it and partook thereof, I exclaimed, Aha, Kasha is our mother, and polenta her daughter! And this is indeed the case; polenta (see *puls pultes*) is nothing other than our Old Slavic kasha, the original preferred food of the ancient Slavs, the remnants of the Slavic-Venetians in Italy."[2]

A special kinship between the Slavs and the ancient Indians and the famous cultural regions in the Orient was also seriously considered. Ignác Jan Hanuš§— the man who once upon a time charmed Božena Němcová with his physique and erudition[3]—in all seriousness related the name Budějovice** to Buddha in his book *Die Wissenschaft des slawischen Mythus.*[4] The Celts simply had to be involved in similar historical confusions.

---

* Stradonice u Berouna and Závist u Zbraslavi are considered the most important Celtic settlements in Bohemia.
† Řehoř Dankovský (1784–1857) and František Šír (1796–1867) were two Czech literary scholars who claimed ancient Greek was a Slavic dialect.
‡ Ján Kollár (1793–1852) was a Slovak poet, prose writer, and Pan-Slavist. His most famous work, *Sláva dcery* (Daughter of Sláva, 1824), a cycle of Petrarchan sonnets glorifying the history of the Slavs and lamenting their present state, made him famous throughout the Slavic world. His posthumously published *Staroitalia slavjanská* (1853), which chronicles his 1841 Italian journey and suggests the ancient Romans were of Slavic ancestry.
§ Ignác Jan Hanuš (1812–69) was a professor of philosophy at the University of Lemberg.
**České Budějovice is a town in southern Bohemia known especially for its beer Budweiser.

It was primarily the poet and priest Karel Vinařický who saw in the Celts an old Slavic tribe, our direct forebears, and he spent many years seeking similarities between Slavic and Gallic names to confirm his theory.[5] After World War I, Jozef Kuffner succumbed to the same passion in his book *Science or Fairy Tale* (1925). For him, too, the Celts are Slavs, and he derived their name from the allegedly erroneous (naturally German) reading of the Slavic designation "čeleď," or domestic servants.[6] In addition, the journalist Pavel Kosatík mentions Kuffner in a 1992 article titled "Strakoš, Chruslav, Chřástal and Those Others or Did our Forefathers Come From the Altai Mountains?" which appeared in the daily *Mladá Fronta Dnes.*[7] Is this a mere anomaly?

Who knows? Today the Celts, popular characters in our Revivalist dreams, have been invoked once again, moreover, in something as practical as a cookbook. Even in the scholarly field, M. C. Putna* has recommended against incorporating Czech studies into Slavic by drawing attention to its Celtic roots. Today, it would not be convincing to suggest that we belong to ancient Greeks and Romans, and it is no longer prestigious to boast of one's Slavic heritage or of a problematic consanguinity with ancient India. "Have you noticed that since the Velvet Revolution we have become more Celtic than Slavic?" asks Aleš Opekar in the daily *Lidové noviny.*[8] The Celts continue to be applicable—or at least it is tempting to apply them, for the Latin name links us to them. Incidentally, during a national search for a name for the western part of Czechoslovakia,† the suggestion *Bohemia* was repeatedly put forward. The Celts help us extend Czech history all the way back to antiquity, and today they strengthen us as we cut ourselves off from Slovakia. At the moment, when the continuity of our national existence seems to be broken by the rupture of Czechoslovak history, the Celts offer a different kind of continuity, one that refers all the way back to mysterious groves of druids above the Vltava River. From this perspective, the Hussite choirs seem to be echoes of ancient Celtic songs, and the affinity for the chalice† is a continuation of "the Celtic search for the proper faith. "And if we are ever beset with doubts about Czech creativity, Czech aversion to violence, faithfulness to ideals, skillfulness and diligence, we can easily cast them away: it is the old creativity, aversion to violence, faithfulness, and diligence of the Celts. To doubt that would surely be foolish.

---

* Martin C. Putna (b. 1968) is professor of comparative literature at Charles University.
† In Czech, the word for the western part of the country is *Čechy.*
‡ The chalice was a Hussite symbol representing their advocacy of Communion in both bread and wine for laypeople.

Notes

SEMIO-FEUILLETONS ON THE END OF EMPIRES

1. Maxim Waldstein, "Tartu Culturology and 'Imperial' Semiotics," in *The Soviet Empire of Signs: A History of the Tartu School of Semiotics* (Saarbrücken, 2008), 161–65 (quotations on 162).

2. Vladimir E. Alexandrov, "Biology, Semiosis, and Cultural Difference in Lotman's Semiosphere," *Comparative Literature* 52.4 (2000): 339–62, esp. 346–47 (quotation on 351).

INTRODUCTION

1. For a full bibliography of Macura's works, see František Knopp, ed., *Bibliografie díla Vladimíra Macury* (Prague, 2000).

2. Macura's friend, the historian Petr Čornej, suggests that this move toward historical studies was inspired personally by Macura's interest in Estonian culture and methodologically by Miroslav Hroch's comparative studies in small European national movements. See Čornej's obituary of Macura in *Český časopis historický* 97.3 (1999): 671–73.

3. The Communist scholarly establishment was very reserved in its reception of the book, which deviated significantly from established wisdom, both methodologically and in its findings. After the fall of Communism in 1989, Czech historiography has become more receptive of Macura's work. See for instance Miroslav Hroch, *Na prahu národní existence* [On the threshold of national existence] (Prague, 1999), 272, as well as the works, among others, of Jiří Rak, Petr Čornej, Zdeněk Hojda, and Jiří Pokorný.

4. Vladimír Macura, "Problems and Paradoxes of the National Revival," in *Bohemia in History*, ed. Mikuláš Teich (Cambridge, UK, 1998), 185.

5. Čornej suggests that Macura's deep and lasting interest in the emergence and shaping of a Czech high culture must be seen also in the context of the depressing atmosphere in "normalized" Czechoslovakia after the Soviet invasion of 1968, when Czech culture seemed very palpably threatened (Čornej, *Český časopis historický*). We can thus see Macura's both critical and loving examination of Czech myths as yet another contribution to a long Czech tradition (made prominent abroad by Milan Kundera) of seeing the Czech national being as something *not* given or self-evident and of questioning its meaning.

6. Macura, "Problems and Paradoxes," 186. See also the first chapter in this book, "Where Is My Home?"

7. Macura, "Problems and Paradoxes," 189.

8. Zdeněk Hrbata provides several apt examples of the different functions of mystifications in the French and Czech contexts in his study *Romantismus a Čechy* [Romanticism and Bohemia] (Jinočany, 1999).

9. Vladimír Macura, *Znamení zrodu* (Jinočany, 1995), 105.

10. This model was essentially ahistorical, just as Soviet style Marxism-Leninism was, in A. J. Polan's words, a philosophy and a politics for the end of time. See A. J. Polan, *Lenin and the End of Politics* (London, 1984).

11. This affinity is crucial also to the argument and analysis in Derek Sayer's *The Coasts of Bohemia: A Czech History* (Princeton, NJ, 1998).

12. On the early history of the movement, see Claire Nolte, *The Sokol in the Czech Lands to 1914: Training for the Nation* (New York, 2002).

13. Milan Zeman et al., eds., *Průvodce po světové literární teorii* (Prague, 1988), 187–92.

14. Again, this observation stems from Čornej.

15. Jaroslav Marek, review of *Masarykovy boty* by Vladimír Macura, *Český časopis historický* 92.1 (1994): 169.

16. In Czech: "*učí buď sličná znamení vzmýšleti, anebo v znameních sličného významu domakávati se*," cited in Vladimír Macura, *Český sen* (Prague, 1998), 187; see also Macura, *Znamení zrodu*, 2.

17. Macura, *Český sen*, 187. These are the final words of the book.

CHAPTER 3. DREAM OF EUROPE

1. Václav Vladivoj Tomek, *Paměti z mého života I* (Prague, 1904), 286–87. See also Vladimír Macura, *Masarykovy boty a jiné semi(o)fejetony* (Prague, 1993), 44–46.

2. Gustáv Kazimír Zechenter-Laskomerský, "Pätdesiat rokov slovenského života, Vlastný životopis," in *Dielo II*, ed. Július Noge (Bratislava, 1988), 93.

3. Václav Bolemír Nebeský, *O literatuře*, ed. Miroslav Heřman (Prague, 1953), 15.

4. Jan Erazim Sojka, "František Palacký," in *Posel z Prahy: Kalendář historický a politický na obyčejný rok 1862*, ed. Karel Sabina (Prague, 1861), 29, repr. in Jan Erazim Sojka, *Naši mužové: Biografie a charakteristiky mužův slovanských* (Prague, 1862), 4.

5. Rudolf Mayer, *Dílo*, ed. František Buriánek (Prague, 1950), 122; Sojka, *Naši mužové*, 4.

6. Tereza Nováková, "Karolína Světlá, její život a spisy," in *Roztroušené kapitoly, vybrané spisy VI*, ed. Věra Vrzalová (Prague, 1961), 146–47.

7. Gustav Pfleger-Moravský, "Pocta Jungmannovi," in *Různé verše: Sebrané spisy III* (Prague, 1877), 219; J. E. K., "Z Králové Dvora," *Lumír* 7 (1857): 981 (a reprinted poem by Václav Hanka).

8. Pim den Boer, "Europe to 1914: The Making of an Idea," in *The History of the Idea of Europe*, What Is Europe 1, ed. Jan van der Dussen and Kevin Wilson (Heerlen, 1993), 13–82.

9. Svatopluk Čech, *Evropa* (Prague, 1886), 5, 43. Originally published in *Lumír* (1878).

10. Svatopluk Čech, *Slavie* (Prague, 1884), 7, 13, 62, 126.

11. Ibid., 63.

12. Georgij Dmitrijevich Gachev, "Amerika v vosprijatii slavianskich pisatelei: Vstrecha nacionalnych obrazov mira," in *Slavianskie i balkanskie kultury XVIII–XIX vv.: Sovetsko-amerikanskii simpozium*, ed. V. I. Zlydnev (Moscow, 1990), 169–80.

13. Sojka, *Naši mužové*, 391.

14. Čech, *Slavie*, 14; "List M. P. Pogodina Fr. Palackému" (unsigned editorial material), *Osvěta* 1 (1871): 44.

15. Maria Bobrowska, "Antyteza słowiańsko-europejska: Z problemów stereotypu," in *Kategoria Europy w kulturach słowiańskich*, ed. Teresa Dąbek-Wirgowa and Andrzej Makowiecki (Warsaw, 1992), 18.

16. Josef Wenzig, *Sebrané spisy II* (Prague, 1874), 18.

17. Jan Helcelet, *Korrespondence a zápisky Jana Helceleta*, ed. Jan Kabelík (Brno, 1910), 432.

18. Anonymous, *Briefe aus Wien von einem Eingeborenen* (Hamburg, 1844), 163.

19. Ivan Skála, *Fronta je všude* (Prague, 1951), 43.

20. Vilém Závada, *Město světla* (Prague, 1951), 10, 33, 31, 35, 24.

21. Jan Pilař, *Radost na zemi* (Prague, 1950), 32.

22. Ctibor Štítnický, *Pochod miliónov* (Bratislava, 1949), 14.

23. Zdeněk Nejedlý, "O Evropě," *Var* 3 (1950/51): 69.

24. H. C. Meyer, *Mitteleuropa in German Thought and Action, 1815–1945* (The Hague, 1955). The theme of Central Europe was asserted between the wars even by Czechoslovak politicians. See Milan Hodža, "Československo a střední Evropa," in *Cesty středoevropskej agrárnej demokracie, 1921–1931*, Články, reči, stúdie 4 (Prague, 1931).

25. Friedrich Naumann, *Mitteleuropa* (Berlin, 1916).

26. Peter Bugge, "The Nation Supreme: The Idea of Europe, 1914–1945," in van der Dussen and Wilson, *The History of the Idea of Europe*, 90.

27. Jan Křen, *Konfliktní společenství: Češi a Němci 1780–1918* (Prague, 1990), 7.

28. Milan Kundera, "Tragédie střední Evropy," *150,000 slov* 10 (1983), cited in *Svědectví* 19.74 (1984/85): 350–51.

29. Jana Klusáková, *Petr Pithart nadoraz* (Prague, 1992), 18.

30. Milan Šimečka, "Jiná civilizace?" *Svědectví* 19.89–90 (1984/85): 313.

31. Milan Šimečka, *Kruhová obrana: Záznamy z roku 1984* (Köln, 1985), 13.

32. Petr Pithart, "Šetřme své dějiny," *Svědectví* 23.89–90 (1984/85): 313.

33. Josef K. [Josef Kroutvor], "Střední Evropa: Torzo omílané historií," *Svědectví* 23.89–90 (1984/85): 261–76, esp. 261, repr. in Josef Kroutvor, *Potíže s dějinami* (Prague, 1990), 49.

34. Vladimír Macura, *Znamení zrodu: České obrození jako kulturní typ* (Prague, 1983), 198–207.

35. Nebeský, *O literatuře*, 35; Jakub Arbes, *Poslední dnové lidstva*, ed. Karel Polák (Prague, 1940), 194; František Jaromír Rubeš, *Deklamovánky a písně III* (Prague, 1839), 16.

36. Milan Kundera, "Český úděl," *Listy* 1.7–8 (1968): 1, 5, repr. in *Svědectví* 19.74 (1984/85): 333–34 (trans. by Tim West).

37. Václav Havel, "Český úděl?" *Tvář* 4.2 (1969): 338–43.

38. Milan Kundera, "Radikalismus a exhibicionismus," *Svědectví* 19.74 (1984/85): 343–49.

39. Václav Havel, *Summer Meditations*, trans. Paul Wilson (Toronto, 1992), 125.

40. Friedrich Ludwig Jahn, *Deutsches Volkstum* (Lübeck, 1810), 14.

41. *Slovenské pohl'ady* 4 (1993): 143; 5: 108; 9: 92; 11: 104–5.

42. *The Baltic States: A Reference Book* (Tallinn, Riga, Vilnius, 1991), 175.

43. Jindřich Vacek, "Na křižovatce kultur: Rozhovor Jindřicha Vacka s Davidem Grossmanem," *Literární noviny* 7.20 (1996): 9.

44. M. Bassin, "Russia Between Europe and Asia: The Ideological Construction of Geographical Space," *Slavic Review* 50 (1991): 1–17. See also Nicolas V. Riasanovsky, "Zrození euroasijství," *Volné sdružení českých rusistů* 9 (1993): 114–19.

CHAPTER 4. THE CENTER

1. J. G. Herder, *Vývoj lidskosti* (Prague, 1941), 15.

2. Ibid., 60, 62.

3. Ibid., 127.

4. On the "center" in mythological systems, see M. Eliade, *Images and Symbols: Studies in Religious Symbolism*, trans. Philip Mairet (London, 1961); M. Eliade, *The Sacred and the Profane: The Nature of Religion*, trans. Willard R. Trask (San Diego, 1987); M. Eliade, *Sacrum, mit historia* (Warsaw, 1974), esp. 31–43, 61–69; and L. Séjourne, *La pensée des anciens mexicains* (Paris, 1966), 90.

5. Josef Jungmann, *Slovesnost* (Prague, 1846), 322–32.

6. Jan Svatopluk Presl, *Savectvo, Rukojet' soustavná k poučení vlastnímu* (Prague, 1834), 106; Jungmann, *Slovesnost*, 375.

7. Josef Jungmann, "Slavěnka Slavinovi," *Prvotiny pěkných umění* 1.17 (1813): 83.

8. Ján Kollár, *Cestopis obsahující cestu do Horní Itálie a odtud přes Tyrolsko a Bavorsko se zvláštním ohledem na slavjanské živly roku 1841 konanou, Se slovníkem slavjanských umělcův všech kmenův* (Prague, 1862), 244.

9. Ibid., 13.

10. Ján Kollár, *Slávy dcera, Lyricko-epická baseň v pěti zpěvích* (Budapest, 1832), 258.

11. *Krok* 1 (1821): 7.

12. František Palacký, *Dějiny národu českého v Čechách a v Moravě dle původních pramenů*, 5 vols. (Prague, 1848), 1:9.

13. Ibid., 1:13.

14. Supplement to *Květy* 13 (1837): 10; František Jaromír Rubeš, *Sebrané spisy*, ed. F. Sekanina (Prague, 1906), 237; Antonín Jaroslav Vrťátko, "Ost und West," supplement to *Květy* 13 (1837): 51.

15. Kollár, *Slávy dcera*, 390.

16. Kollár, *Cestopis*, 260; F. L. Jahn, *Deutsches Volkstum* (Leipzig, 1817), 11.

17. A similar image was asserted even in such ephemeral statements as "Prague lies between Dresden and Vienna; Dresden is a city of art, Vienna of naturalness. Prague, however, embraces both art and naturalness, and this union kindles and develops musical abilities" (*Květy* 13 [1837]: 161).

18. Štěpán Launer, *Povaha Slovanstva se zvláštním ohledem na spisovní řeč Čechů, Moravanů, Slezáků a Slováků* (Leipzig, 1847); C. Cochia, "Ohlas proti Ohlášení," *Orol tatranský* 3 (1847): 76, 606.

19. Josef Jungmann, *Boj o obrození národa,* ed. F. Vodička (Prague, 1948), 68.

20. Ján Kollár, *Výklad čili přímětky a vysvětlivky ku Slávy dceře* (Prague, 1862), 4.

21. Ján Kollár, *Hlasové o potřebě jednoty spisovného jazyka pro Čechy, Moravany a Slováky* (Prague, 1846), 156.

22. Ján Kollár, *Prózy, Vybrané spisy II,* ed. F. R. Tichý (Prague, 1956), 219.

23. Augustin Smetana, *Sebrané spisy I,* ed. M. Bayerová (Prague, 1960), 143.

24. Miroslav Jozef Hurban, "Veda a Slovenské pohľady," *Slovenské pohľady* 1 (1846): 9.

25. Peter Kellner-Hostinský [Peter Pavel Kellner], "Otvorený list p. Ctibohovi Cochiusovi," *Orol tatranský* 2 (1847): 467–69, 476–78, 483–86.

26. Ibid., 467.

27. Kollár, *Prózy,* 255.

Chapter 5. Prague

1. Antonín Jaroslav Puchmajer, *Sebrání básní a zpěvů I* (Prague, 1795), 78; Václav Thám, *Básně v řeči vázané,* ed. V. Brtník (Prague, 1916), 37.

2. Karel Hynek Mácha, *Próza, Spisy II,* ed. K. Janský, R. Skřeček, and K. Dvořák (Prague, 1961), 110.

3. References are to A. Bäuerle, *Ausgewählte Werke,* vol. 1, *Aline oder Wien in einem anderen Weltteile* (Vienna, 1913), and J. N. Štěpánek, *Alina aneb Praha v jiném dílu světa* (Prague, 1825).

4. Bäuerle, *Ausgewählte Werke,* 1:95; Štěpánek, *Alina aneb Praha v jiném dílu světa,* 12.

5. Štěpánek, *Alina aneb Praha v jiném dílu světa,* 9, 22.

6. Bäuerle, *Ausgewählte Werke,* 1:90, 105.

7. See Josef Kajetán Tyl, *Kusy mého srdce,* ed. M. Otruba (Prague, 1952), 385.

8. Ján Kollár, *Slávy dcera, Lyricko-epická baseň v pěti zpěvích* (Budapest, 1832), 237.

9. On general Romantic characteristics, especially the iconography of the "castle," "king," and "grave," see Z. Hrbata, "Symbolika hradu v Chateaubriandových Pamětech ze záhrobí: Combourg a Pražský hrad," in *Ročenka Kruhu moderních filologů* (Prague, 1983), 14–25.

10. Václav Hanka, *Písně a Prostonárodní srbská múza do Čech převedená,* ed. J. Máchal (Prague, 1918), 191.

11. František Turinský, *Záviš Vítkovec z Růží, Básnické spisy* (Prague, 1880), 372.

12. Josef Linda, *Záře nad pohanstvem nebo Václav a Boleslav* (Prague, 1818), 73.

13. See entries for "hora" (gora), "strom života" (drevo zhizni), and "kosmický strom" (drevo mirovoye) by V. N. Toporov in *Mify narodov mira: Sovetskaya Entsiklopediya,*

vol. 1, ed. S. A. Tokarev (Moscow, 1980), 311–15, 396–406. See also V. N. Toporov, "l'Albero universale: Saggio d'interpretazione semiotica," in *Ricerche semiotiche: Nuove tendenze delle scienze umane nell'URSS*, ed. Jurij M. Lotman and Boris A. Uspenskij, trans. Clara S. Janovič (Torino, 1973), 148–201; M. Eliade, *Images and Symbols: Studies in Religious Symbolism* (London, 1961).

14. Tyl, *Kusy mého srdce*, 382.

15. Toporov, *Mify narodov mira*, 1:314.

16. František Palacký, *Básně*, ed. J. Jakubec (Prague, 1898), 45.

17. On the motivations of consecrating the city as an important center of awakening national life, see K. Krejčí, *Praha legend a skutečnosti* (Prague, 1981), 170–200.

18. See the valuable study by S. Mečiar, *Tatry v slovenskej a pol'skej poezii* (Turčiansky Sväty Martin, 1932).

19. Miloslav Jozef Hurban, "Slovensko a jeho život literárny," *Slovenské pohl'ady* 1 (1846): 19.

20. H. Janaszek-Ivaničková, "Mit szturowski wczoraj i dziś," *Pamietnik slowiański* 26 (1976): 65–93.

21. On the origin and representation of the modern metropolis myth, see R. Caillois, *Le Mythe et l'homme* (Paris, 1938).

22. D. Hodrová discusses Prague as a city of disillusionment in the Czech novel during the turn of the century in *Město v české kultuře 19. Století*, ed. Milena Freimanová (Prague, 1983), 168–77.

CHAPTER 7. THE POTATO BUG

1. "Provolání vlády k boji proti mandelince bramborové," *Rudé právo* 30.153, 29 June 1950, 1.

2. "Americká loutková vláda v Jižní Koreji zahájila ozbrojený útok proti korejské lidové republice," *Rudé právo* 30.151, 20 June 1950, 2.

3. Jiří Kubka, "Americký brouk," *Lidové noviny* 58.161, 12 July 1950, 3.

4. Arnold Kac and Jiří Foltýn, *Americký brouk* (Prague, 1950), 26, 5.

5. *Dikobraz* 6.30 (1950): 4.

6. Zikmund Skyba, "Gangsteři v letadlech," *Lidové noviny* 58.153, 1 July 1950, 26.

7. *Lidové noviny* 58.159, 9 July 1950, 7.

8. Ondřej Sekora, *O zlém brouku Bramborouku, O mandelince americké, která chce loupit z našich talířů* (Prague, 1950).

9. Kamil Winter, "Pokus imperialistů o ohrožení naší úrody," *Rudé právo* 30.154, 30 June 1950, 2.

10. Karel Bradáč, "Ze života hmyzu," *Dikobraz* 6.31 (1950): 5.

11. Václav Lacina, "Mandelinka bramborová," *Lidové noviny* 58.164, 15 July 1950, 4.

12. Jiří Valja, "Coloradský brouk a ukrajinský letčik," *Lidové noviny* 58.181, 4 July 1950, 1–2; Kubka, "Americký brouk."

13. *Rudé právo* 30.155, 1 July 1950, 7.

14. Jiří Foltýn and Arnold Kac, *Do boje proti americkému brouku* (Bratislava, 1951), 20.

15. Lacina, "Mandelinka bramborová."

16. "Nový spojenec Američanů," *Rudé právo* 30.163, 12 July 1950, 3.

17. Sekora, *O zlém brouku Bramborouku.*

18. "Nový spojenec Američanů."

19. Josef Kainar, *Český sen* (Prague, 1953), 33.

20. Skyba, "Gangsteři v letadlech," 1.

21. K. Bradáč, "Ze života hmyzu."

22. *Rudé právo* 30.163, 12 July 1950, 3.

23. SK [Jan Skácel], *Rovnost* 159, 9 July 1950, 4.

24. "Pracující měst a venkova společně hubí amerického brouka," *Rudé právo* 30.166, 15 July 1950, 5.

25. Kubka, "Americký brouk."

26. "Brambor vzdorující mandelince," *Květy* 1.21 (1951): 11.

27. Valja, "Coloradský brouk a ukrajinský letčik," 2.

28. Miroslav Kárný, "Americké Gestapo hledá Fučíka," *Rudé právo* 31.9, 11 January 1951, 5.

CHAPTER 8. DEATH OF THE LEADER

1. Vilém Závada, "Civilizace smrti" (Civilization of Death), in *Město světla* (Prague, 1950), 30–31.

2. Jan Alois Uher, in *Žijí v nás: Sborník básní a skladeb lidových autorů a skladatelů k úmrtí J. V. Stalina a Klementa Gottwalda,* ed. Pavel Hanuš (Prague, 1954), 59.

3. Stanislav Oborský, "Ze životopisu," in *Gottwald je s námi, Náš první dělnický prezident v zrcadle české a slovenské poesie a prózy,* ed. Alexej Kusák (Prague, 1953), 270.

4. Jan Pilař, *Hvězda života: Verše z let 1950–1953* (Prague, 1953), 107; Marie Lašková, in Hanuš, *Žijí v nás,* 23.

5. Josef Návrat, "Ještěs nám neměl odcházet!" in Hanuš, *Žijí v nás,* 41; Zdeněk Sýkora, "Nevím," in Hanuš, *Žijí v nás,* 42.

6. Pavel Kohout, "Čas lásky a boje," in Pavel Kohout, *Verše a písně z let 1952–1954* (Prague, 1954), 55; Ludmila Zembalová, "Pamatuj, synku," in Hanuš, *Žijí v nás,* 55; Josef Záhořík, "Hlas," in Hanuš, *Žijí v nás,* 85.

7. Ján Kostra, "Proti smrti," in Kusák, *Gottwald je s námi,* 295.

8. Václav Daněk, "Soudruhu Staline!" in Hanuš, *Žijí v nás,* 43.

9. Zdena Wolkerová, "Stalin mrtev," in Hanuš, *Žijí v nás,* 17.

10. Anon., "Sovětský lid a všechno pokrokové lidstvo se loučí se svým učitelem a otcem—soudruhem Stalinem," *Rudé právo* 33.67, 8 March 1953, 1; Anon., "Československý lid se loučí s Klementem Gottwaldem," *Rudé právo* 33.76, 17 March 1953, 1.

11. Jiří Marek, "Ve Španělském sále," *Rudé právo* 33.76, 17 March 1953, 1.

12. Jan Drda, "Národ před rakví otcovou," *Rudé právo* 33.77, 18 March 1953, 3.

13. Boris Groys, *Gesamtkunstwerk Stalin, Die gespaltene Kultur in der Sowjetunion* (Munich, Vienna, 1988), 71–76.

14. Jiří Havel, "Kupředu, soudruzi," in Kusák, *Gottwald je s námi,* 355.

15. Kohout, "Čas lásky a boje," 61.

CHAPTER 9. SYMBOL WITH A HUMAN FACE

1. Charles William Morris, "Základy teorie znaků," in *Lingvistické čítanky I, Sémiotikas*, vol. 2 (Prague, 1970), 7–55.
2. Václav Havel, *Lidové noviny*, 9 November 1992.
3. Roman Kováč, "Alexander Dubček zemřel," *Rudé právo*, 9 November 1992, 1–2.
4. Čestmír Císař, "Skromný politik," *Rudé právo*, 9 November 1992, 2.
5. Bohumil Hrabal, "Večerníček pro Cassia," *Lidové noviny*, 10 November 1992.
6. Břetislav Rychlík, "Co my už s Bílakem," *Lidové noviny*, 14 November 1992.
7. *Sedm pražských dnů, 21.–27. Srpen 1968, Dokumentace* (Prague, 1990), 234.
8. Ladislav Ťažký, "Zlomený kvet českej a slovenskej jari," *Slobodný piatok*, 13 November 1992, 7.
9. Zdeněk Mlynář, "Člověk a symbol," *Rudé právo*, 9 November 1992, 3.
10. "Zemřel Alexander Dubček," *Lidová demokracie*, 2 February 1992, 1.

CHAPTER 10. THE METRO

1. Miroslav Červenka, "Semiotika," in *Předpoklady a meze využití podzemí*, manuscript of a collection of material from a conference on the history and theory of architecture at the National Technical Museum, 19 February 1976.
2. Petr Skarlant, *Mimoúrovňové křižovatky* (Prague, 1980), 58.
3. Jan Rejžek, *Hodina angličtiny, Nic Moc* (Prague, 1980), 48.
4. Lubomír Brožek, "Tři básně z metra," in *Kolotoč aneb Malá Grand Prix* (Prague, 1985), 43.
5. Miroslav Florian, *Zelená flétna* (Prague, 1979), 44; Jiří Žáček, *Text-appeal* (Prague, 1986), 31.
6. Ivo Šmoldas, "Čtenáři v metru," in *Zvláštní znamení*, ed. Ladislav Verecký (Prague, 1985), 92.
7. Brožek, "Tři básně z metra," 42.
8. Florian, *Zelená flétna*.
9. Brožek, "Tři básně z metra," 45.
10. Jiří Žáček, *Kolik má Praha věží* (Prague, 1984), 30; Josef Rumler, "Na Gottwaldově mostě," in *Týž, Výstup na horu Říp* (Hradec Králové, 1978), 72.
11. Josef Šimon, *Český den* (Prague, 1979), 11.
12. Brožek, "Tři básně z metra," 43.
13. Šimon, *Český den*.
14. Šmoldas, "Čtenáři v metro."
15. Skarlant, *Mimoúrovňové křižovatky*, 60.
16. Evžen Kyllar, "Architektonické a výtvarné řešení stanic," *Zpravodaj Metro* 16.3 (1985): 97.
17. Josef Václav Frič, "U stop Dantova náhrobku v Santa Croce," in *Písně z bašty a jiné básně* (Prague, 1952), 183; Jan Neruda, "Písně kosmické," in *Básně, Spisy* 2 (Prague, 1956), 38.
18. Josef Miloslav Hurban, *Cesta Slováka ku bratrům českým na Moravě a v Čechách* (Pešť, 1841), 11.

19. Pravoslav Trojan Knovízský, "Příjezd prvního parostroje," *Květy* 12.94 (1845): 94.

20. Karel Šmídek, "Z Moravy, Železná dráha," *Květy* 6.2 (1839): 15–16.

21. Lalka Velková, "Trasa C—nastupujte!" *Květy* 24.18 (1974): 15–16.

22. Mikuláš Lacek, "Význam metra pro rozvoj městské hromadné dopravy," in *Rozvoj systemů městské hromadné dopravy*, ed. Miroslav Foglar (Prague, 1989), 77.

23. Jiří Schwaller, quoted in *Všechna metra světa*, ed. Josef Křivánek, Zbyněk Šmíd, and Jaromír Vítek (Prague, 1986), 109.

24. Bohuslav Blažek, *Venkov města média* (Prague, 1998), 169.

25. Červenka, "Semiotika."

26. Blažek, "Metro jako sociální jev," unpublished manuscript.

27. Gavriil Petrosjan, "Sovětský Ikarus," *Rudé právo* 58.54, 6 March 1978, 2

28. Anonymous, "Společná cesta vesmírem," *Práce* 34.54, 4 March 1978, 2.

29. Petrosjan, "Sovětský Ikarus," 2.

30. Lacek, "Význam metra pro rozvoj městské hromadné dopravy," 73.

31. Rumler, "Na Gottwaldově mostě," 72.

32. Blažek, "Metro."

33. Julius Fučík describes the Moscow metro in a similarly dramatic fashion (Julius Fučík, "Stručné dějiny moskevského metra," in *V zemi milované, Reportáže ze Sovětského svazu* [Prague, 1949], 203–4). First, he presents the negative views of foreign specialists who have studied the geological map of the area and determined that it would be impossible to build a metro given such conditions. Then he continues: "Comrade Stalin also looked at the geological map of Moscow and without blinking an eye said, "There is no fortress that the Bolsheviks cannot conquer."

34. Miroslav Florian, *Sluneční vítr* (Prague, 1984), 269.

35. Blažek, "Metro."

Chapter 11. Michurin

1. Karel Šiktanc, *Tobě, živote! Verše* (Prague, 1951), 43; Ctibor Štítnický, *Jarná piesen družstevníka* (Prague, 1950), 50.

2. Milan Lajčiak, "Súdružka moja zem," in *Verše* (Bratislava, 1953), 44; Vítězslav Nezval, *Křídla, Básně z let 1949–1952* (Prague, 1952), 23.

3. Jan Kozák, *Adam a Eva* (Prague, 1982), 12.

4. Ibid., 231–32.

5. Dmitrii Likhachev, "Slovo i sad," in *Finitis Duodecim Lustris: Sbornik statei k 60-letiiu Prof. Iu. M. Lotmana*, ed. S. G. Isakov (Talinn, 1982), 57–65.

6. Aleksandr Dovzhenko, *Zhizn v tsvetu* (Moscow, 1949), 6.

7. Ibid., 39.

8. A. J. Molodčikov, *Člověk mění přírodu* (Prague, 1950), 94.

9. Ivan Turgenev, *Fathers and Sons*, trans. Peter Carson (New York, 2009), 43.

10. Dovzhenko, *Zhizn v tsvetu*, 79.

11. Alena Bernášková, "Vítězství nejkrásnější," *Květy* 2.1 (1952): 5.

12. Josef Rybák, "Ta doba je v nás," *Květy* 2 (1952): 3.

13. Jean Varloot, "Živý Balzac," *Var* 3.4–5 (1950–51): 135.

14. For further developments in agricultural science, see *Za další rozvoj zemědělské vědy: První výroční valné shromáždění Československé Akademie Zemědělských věd* (Prague, 1954), 41–42.

15. Vjačeslav Lebeděv, *Povídky o Mičurinovi* (Prague, 1951), 8.

16. Miroslav Červenka, *Po stopách zítřka* (Prague, 1953), 52, 63; Jiří Taufer, "Cesta do SSSR," in *Básnický almanach*, ed. Vilém Závada (Prague, 1953), 55.

17. Šiktanc, *Tobě, živote! Verše*, 37.

18. Jan Pilař, *Radost na zemi* (Prague, 1950), 42; Pavel Kohout, "Verše a písně," in *Tři knihy veršů* (Prague, 1955), 42.

19. Stanislav Neumann, *Píseň o lásce a nenávisti* (Prague, 1952), 23.

20. Lajčiak, "Súdružka moja zem," 29; Stanislav Neumann, *Píseň o Stalinu* (Prague, 1950), 14.

21. Miloslav Bureš, from the cycle of poems "Všechno mi připomíná píseň," in Závada, *Básnický almanach*, 74.

22. Lebeděv, *Povídky o Mičurinovi*, 28.

23. Václav Daněk, "Soudruhu Staline!" in *Žijí v nás: Sborník básní a skladeb lidových autorů a skladatelů k úmrtí J. V. Stalina a Klementa Gottwalda*, ed. Pavel Hanuš and Karel Mlčoch (Prague, 1954), 43.

24. Jan Pilař, "Hvězda života," in *Hvězda života: Verše z let 1950–1953* (Prague, 1953), 112.

CHAPTER 12. SPARTAKIAD

1. Vilém Mucha, *První celostátní spartakiáda 1955—věcí všeho pracujícího lidu Československa* (Prague, 1955), 16.

2. Marie Zemanová, *Politicko-výchovnou prací přispějeme k úspěchu I. celostátní spartakiády* (Prague, 1954), 9.

3. Alexej Čepička, quoted in Zemanová, *Politicko-výchovnou prací*, 5, 15.

4. Lieutenant General František Janda, head of the State Committee for Physical Education and Sports, quoted in Zemanová, *Politicko-výchovnou prací*, 34.

5. Klement Gottwald, "Sokolstvo v budování lidově demokratické republiky," in *Lví silou, Pocta a dík Sokolstvu* (Prague, 1948), 11.

6. Václav Kopecký, "Sokol a Slovanstvo," in *Lví silou*, 15.

7. Eva Stehlíková, "Obřadní a divadelní prvky v sokolském hnutí," in *Divadlo v české kultuře 19. století*, ed. Milena Freimanová (Prague, 1985), 161–66.

8. "Projev prezidenta republiky soudruha Antonína Zápotockého," *Rudé právo* 35.2, 3 January 1955, 1.

9. "Krása i zbraň," *Obrana lidu* 14.158, 2 July 1955, 1.

10. "Projev prezidenta republiky Antonína Zápotockého," *Rudé právo* 35.173, 24 June 1955, 1.

11. Petr Fidelius, *Jazyk a moc* (Munich, 1983).

12. Jana Štroblová, "Až všechna srdce zazní," *Mladá fronta* 11.159, 2 July 1955, 1.

13. František Kožík, "Živé pohlednice ze Strahova," *Večerní Praha* 1.82, 4 July 1955, 3.

14. Jan Kopecký, "Pohled do hlediště," *Rudé právo* 35.182, 3 July 1955, 3.

15. Jan Kopecký, "To byl příspěvek do diskuse!" *Literární noviny* 4.28, 9 July 1955, 2.

16. Pavel Kohout, "Chvála tvořivých záloh," *Rudé právo* 35.179, 30 June 1955, 1.

17. Jiřina Dumasová, "Vzácný květ," *Zemědělské noviny* 11.153, 25 June 1955, 3.

18. Ladislav Štoll, *Politický smysl Sokolství* (Prague, 1932), 5.

19. Sergej Machonin, "Tvář našeho času," *Literární noviny* 4.27 (1955): 2.

20. Jarmila Urbánková, "Cvičení žen s kuželem," *Literární noviny* 4.26 (1955): 1.

21. Ladislav Ježek, "Z dopisu ČSL rozhlasu," in Mucha, *První celostátní spartakiáda 1955*, 142.

22. "Krása i zbraň," 1.

23. Vladimír Šacha, "Prahou okouzleni," *Učitelské noviny* 5.29–30 (1955): 5.

24. Marie Majerová, "Chvála spartakiády," in Mucha, *První celostátní spartakiáda 1955*, 7–8.

25. Mucha, *První celostátní spartakiáda 1955*, 17.

26. Jiřina Dumasová, "Vlajky vylétly opět na stožár," *Zemědělské noviny* 11.160, 3 July 1955, 2.

27. Jiří Navrátil, "Zpěv o dnešním dnu," *Mladá fronta* 11.160, 3 July 1955, 1.

28. Miroslav Florian, "Spartakiádní," *Literární noviny* 4.26 (1955): 1.

29. Arne Hirdman, *Literární noviny* 4.28 (1955): 2.

30. "Tristan Tzara v Československu," *Literární noviny* 4.27 (1955): 3. See also "Co o ní řekli, Byla úchvatná," *Mladá fronta* 11.163, 7 July 1955, 4.

CHAPTER 14. MINUS-STALIN

1. Yuri M. Lotman, *The Structure of the Artistic Text*, trans. Gail Lenhoff and Ronald Vroon (Ann Arbor, 1977), 95.

2. Petr Volf, "Bude opět oživen metronom?" *Mladá fronta Dnes*, 4 September 1992; "Zůstane metronom nad Prahou?" *Mladá fronta Dnes*, 5 September 1992, 7.

CHAPTER 15. THE CELTS WITHIN US

1. *Velká česká kuchařka* (Prague, 1992), 7.

2. Ján Kollár, *Cestopis obsahující cestu do Horní Itálie* (Prague, 1862), 56.

3. Božena Němcová, *Listy I, Spisy B. Němcové 12* (Prague, 1951), 144.

4. Ignác Jan Hanuš, *Die Wissenschaft des slawischen Mythus* (Lemberg, Stanislawów, and Tarnów, 1842), 90.

5. Karel Vinařický, *Korespondence a spisy pamětní II* (Prague, 1909).

6. Jozef Kuffner, *Věda či báchora? Paběrky k otázce slovanského dávnověku* (Prague, 1925).

7. Pavel Kosatík, "Strakoš, Chruslav, Chřástal a ti druzí aneb Přišli naši tatínkové z Altaje?" *Mladá fronta Dnes*, 31 December 1992, 7.

8. Aleš Opekar, "Slovansko-keltské objevování," *Lidové noviny*, 22 January 1993, 13.

Further Readings

WORKS BY VLADIMÍR MACURA

České Obrození jako kulturní typ [The Czech National Revival as a cultural type]. Prague, 1992.

"Culture as Translation." In *Translation, History, and Culture*, edited by Susan Bassnett and André Lefevere, 64–70. New York, 1990.

"Identita a identity" [Identity and identities]. Review of Robert B. Pynsent, *Questions of Identity: Czech and Slovak Ideas of Nationality and Personality* (Budapest, 1994). *Tvar* 5.9 (5 May 1994): 5.

"Lotmanův koncept sémiosféry a 'jiná' dekonstrukce" [Lotman's concept of semiosphere and other deconstruction]. *Slovenská literatura* 41.5–6 (1994): 464–69.

Masarykovy boty a jiné semi(o)fejetony [Masaryk's boots and other semi(o)-sketches]. Prague, 1993.

"Mýty dneška, slovenské i české" [The myths of today, Slovak and Czech]. *Tvar* 4.47/48 (1993).

"Na slovo s Jurijom Lotmanom" [A word with Yuri Lotman]. *Slovenské pohlady* 108.2 (1992): 94–97.

Šťastný věk: symboly, emblémy a mýty 1948–1989 [The joyous age: Symbols, emblems and myths, 1948–1989]. Prague, 1992.

Znamení zrodu: České národni obrození jako kulturní typ [Sign(s) of the birth: The Czech National Revival as a cultural type]. 2nd ed. Jinočany, 1995.

OTHER SUGGESTED READINGS

Cravens, Craig. *The Culture and Customs of the Czech Republic and Slovakia*. Westport, CT, 2006.

Crowley, David, and Susan Reid. *Socialist Spaces: Sites of Everyday Life in the Eastern Bloc*. Oxford, UK: 2002.

Demetz, Peter. *Prague in Black and Gold: Scenes from the Life of a European City*. New York, 1997.

Hahnová, Eva. "Sémiotika Evropy" [The semiotics of Europe]. In *Evropa očima Čechů* [Europe through Czech Eyes], ed. Eva Hahnová. Prague, 1997.

Havel, Václav, et al. *The Power of the Powerless: Citizens against the State in Central-Eastern Europe*, edited by John Keane. Armonk, NY, 1985.

Hodrová, Daniela. *Poetika míst: kapitoly z literární tematologie* [The poetics of places: Chapters from literary thematology]. Jinočany, 1997.

Kollár, Ján. *Reciprocity between the Various Tribes and Dialects of the Slavic Nation*, translated and edited by Alexander Maxwell. Bloomington, IN, 2008.

Ripellino, Angelo Maria. *Prague in Black and Gold*. New York, 1997.

Sayer, Derek. *The Coasts of Bohemia: A Czech History*. Princeton, NJ, 1998.

Index